soft furnishings
& DESIGNER TRIMS

Cole's Home Library Craftbooks
Glen Ellen, California

CONTENTS

WHITE BED LINEN SET

We used a damask fabric for this linen set and calculated fabric quantities using the most economical cutting method. Allow extra for patterned fabric with one-way design.

Also, because mattress sizes vary, it is important to measure your mattress before purchasing fabrics. Maximum width of sheeting fabric is usually 98 inches; you may be able to find wider fabric, which is preferable if you are making sheets for queen and king beds.

Flat Sheet with Lace Inset

3 yards x 72"-wide or 90"-wide sheeting (for twin bed)
3 yards x 90"-wide sheeting (for full bed)
3 yards x 98"-wide sheeting (for queen bed)
3 1/4 yards x 98"-wide sheeting (for king bed)
2 1/2"-wide double edge Battenburg lace
thread

Finished size (width x length): Twin 72" x 100"; full 90" x 100"; queen 105" x 98"; king 109" x 98".

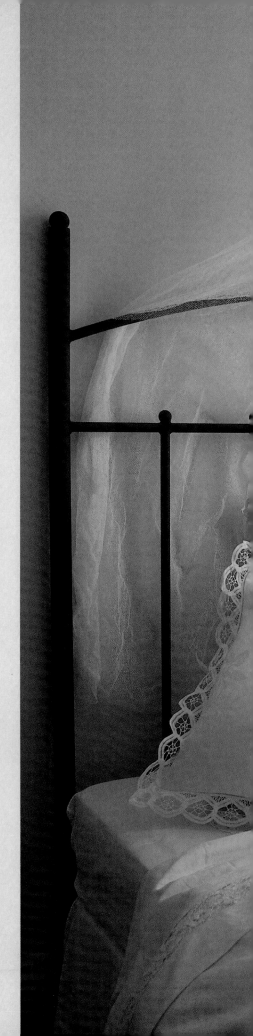

BED LINEN

Luxurious bed linen can be yours for little cost, by using inexpensive, appealing cotton fabrics, and making it requires only a minimum of sewing skill. We give instructions for all the basics: fitted sheets, flat sheets, quilt covers and pillowcases. You will need to use sheeting or very wide fabric for the sheets, but pillowcases can be made from almost any fabric, provided that it is comfortable against the skin and launders well. Also included are tips on how to decorate pillowcases, personalize a quilt cover and brighten a room with an easy bed canopy or padded headboard.

Cut fabric for sheet: twin 72″ (or 71″ if using 71″-wide sheeting) x 104″; full 90″ x 104″; queen 105″ x 98″; king 109½″ x 98″.

Neaten raw edges, then press under and stitch ⅜-inch hems on all edges of sheet. Cut lace to fit width of sheet, plus ¾ inch. Hem each end of lace.

For twin and full sheets:

Turn under and stitch another 2¾ inches at upper edge and another ¾ inch at lower edge. Pin lace across upper edge of sheet, on right side, just below 2¾-inch hem. Stitch around all edges of lace using close zigzag stitch. Carefully cut fabric away from behind lace.

For queen and king sheets:

Cut off a 4-inch-wide strip across sheet top. Spread sheet and 7-inch strip 2 inches apart, and pin lace between fabric pieces, over raw edges. Stitch in place using close zigzag stitch. Turn over 2 inches to wrong side on top edge of sheet, stitch in place. (If 102-inch-wide sheeting is available, queen and king sheets can be made as for full.)

Fitted Sheet

☙ *1¼ yards x 90″-wide sheeting (for twin bed)*
☙ *2 yards x 90″-wide sheeting (for full bed)*
☙ *2¼ yards x 98″-wide sheeting (for queen bed)*
☙ *2½ yards x 98″-wide sheeting (for king bed)*
☙ *¼″-wide elastic*
☙ *thread*

To fit mattress size (width x length x depth): Twin 35″ x 73½″ x 8″; full 54″ x 73½″ x 8″; queen 60″ x 80″ x 8″; king 71½″ x 80″ x 8″.

Note: Mattress sizes vary. To calculate correct sheet size, multiply the mattress depth by two and add this measurement, plus desired tuck-in allowance, to mattress length and width measurements. ⅜-inch seam allowance is included in lengths given.

Mark an 8-inch square at each corner of sheet. Cut out each square. With right sides together, pin and stitch along cut edges *(see diagram 1)*. Trim and zigzag seam allowances.

Zigzag raw edges of sheet, then press under ⅜ inch all around to form a casing. Stitch along casing edge, leaving an opening in stitching at each corner.

Cut two pieces of elastic the width of the mattress. Thread elastic pieces through casing at the top and bottom of sheet *(see diagram 2)*. Secure ends of elastic with zigzag. Slip-stitch openings closed.

DIAGRAM 1

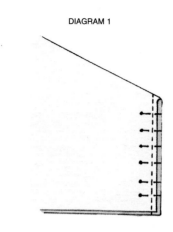

DIAGRAM 2

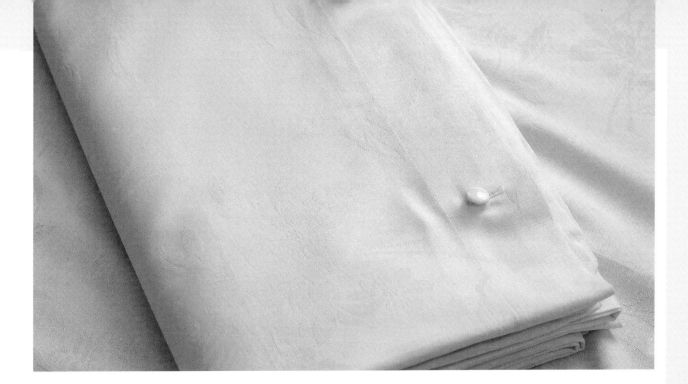

Quilt Cover

🌿 *3 1/4 yards x 90"-wide sheeting (for twin bed)*
🌿 *4 yards x 90"-wide sheeting (for full bed)*
🌿 *4 3/4 yards x 90"-wide sheeting (for queen bed)*
🌿 *5 1/2 yards x 90"-wide sheeting (for king bed)*
🌿 *eight buttons*   🌿 *thread*

Finished size (width x length): Twin 55" x 82"; full 71 1/2" x 82"; queen 82" x 82"; king 96" x 82".

Cut two fabric pieces for cover: Twin 56 1/2" x 87"; full 72" x 87"; queen 83" x 87"; king 97" x 87". 3/8-inch seam allowance is included.

Turn in and stitch a 3/8-inch hem along one short end of each piece for twin, full and queen cover, and along one long end of each piece for king cover.

Pin top to bottom cover, right sides facing and matching hemmed edges. Stitch around three raw edges. Trim and zigzag seam allowances. Turn right side out, press.

Turn under another 2 3/8 inches along bottom edge, top-stitch hem. Make eight evenly spaced buttonholes along hemmed edge of cover top, sew buttons on cover bottom to correspond.

European Pillowcase with Lace Trim

🌿 *3/4 yard x 60"-wide fabric*
🌿 *4 yards x 4"-wide single edge Battenburg lace*
🌿 *2 1/2 yards x 2 1/2"-wide double edge Battenburg lace*
🌿 *thread*

Finished size: 26"-square plus lace.

Cut one 27-inch-square piece fabric for front. Cut one 27" x 18" piece and one 27" x 15" piece for back. Cut four 34-inch pieces single edge lace and four 22-inch pieces double edge lace. 3/8-inch seam allowance is included.

Turn under and stitch a 3/8-inch hem along one 27-inch edge of each back piece. Turn under another 3/8 inch on each piece and top-stitch. Overlap large back piece over small back piece until 67" square; baste sides together.

Pin and stitch single edge lace pieces, right sides together, mitering, or dovetailing, corners (as shown in Pillowcase with Lace Edging, ***diagram 1***, on page 8). Pin and stitch lace around front, raw edges and right sides together (as shown in Pillowcase with Lace Edging, ***diagram 2***).

With right sides together, stitch double edge lace pieces together to form a square, mitering, or dovetailing, corners as before. Pin lace square to front pillowcase approximately 4 inches in from edge, zigzag or slip-stitch in position.

With right sides together, pin back to front, over lace. Stitch, trim and zigzag seam allowances. Remove basting, turn right side out.

Pillowcase with Lace Edging

🍃 *1 1/4 yards x 45"-wide or*
20" x 72"-wide fabric
🍃 *3 1/3 yards x 2 1/2"-wide single edge*
Battenburg lace
🍃 *thread*

Finished size: Approximately 29" x 19" plus lace edge.

Cut one 30" x 20" piece fabric for front and one 31 1/2" x 20" piece fabric for back. Cut one 20" x 8" piece fabric for flap. Cut two 35-inch and two 25-inch pieces lace. 3/8-inch seam allowance is included.

Stitch lace pieces together at ends to form a rectangle to fit around front, dovetailing, or mitering, corners as shown in *diagram 1*. With right sides and raw edges together, pin and stitch lace around front *(see diagram 2)*.

Press under a 3/4-inch hem along one 20-inch edge of flap piece, then turn under another 3/4 inch and top-stitch double hem in place. With right sides together, stitch flap to front along one 20-inch edge.

Press under a 3/4-inch hem along one 20-inch edge of back piece, then turn under another 3/4 inch and top-stitch double hem in place.

With right sides together, pin back to front around raw edges. Fold flap around to back at open end of pillowcase, right side of flap against wrong side of back, aligning raw edges. Stitch side and lower edges of pillowcase, trim and zigzag seam allowances. Turn right side out.

DIAGRAM 1

DIAGRAM 2

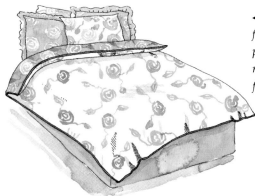

◀ *A reversible coverlet, made in contrasting fabric front and back, offers the option of two moods for the price of one. Add a cluster of pillows using the same mix of materials and highlight the juxtaposition of fabrics with a contrasting piped edging.*

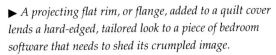

▶ *A projecting flat rim, or flange, added to a quilt cover lends a hard-edged, tailored look to a piece of bedroom software that needs to shed its crumpled image.*

◀ *A piece of fabric is a versatile medium. Depending on how it is put to use, the same design can produce some surprisingly different effects. A flat expanse of restful linear check made into a quilt cover metamorphoses into a much busier design when used for a ruffled trim. The addition of piping in a contrasting color divides and accentuates the differences.*

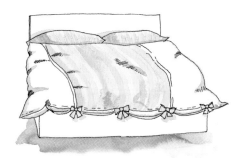

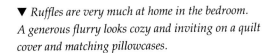

▼ *Ruffles are very much at home in the bedroom. A generous flurry looks cozy and inviting on a quilt cover and matching pillowcases.*

▲ *Snaps and zippers have their place (usually out of sight), but a fastening can easily be turned into a design feature. Keep a coverlet in place by using matching or contrasting bow ties, and turn something functional into something special.*

Also note the clever piecing of fabric, eliminating the use of sheeting-width fabric.

QUILT COVERS

CHECKED QUILT AND PILLOWCASES

Quilt Cover

This quilt cover opens from the top edge, with a buttoned overlap on the upper side.

❧ 5 3/4 yards x 45"-wide,
or 3 3/4 yards x 60"-wide blue gingham
❧ 3 yards x 80"-wide white cotton sheeting
❧ 1/3 yard x 45"-wide tiny-checked blue gingham
❧ 7 2/3 yards x 5/8"-wide Swiss embroidery or eyelet
lace, with entredeux edge
❧ 2 1/4 yards x 1 1/4"-wide zigzag-edged eyelet lace
❧ four buttons

Finished size: 78"-square (for full or queen quilt).

From blue gingham, cut five strips, each 65 1/2" x 16". From joining trim, cut four 65 1/2-inch long strips. From white sheeting, cut a 2 1/2 yard x 2 1/4 yard rectangle for backing and overlap, and a 14" x 79" strip for the upper edge of the quilt top. From tiny-checked gingham, cut two 6-inch-wide strips. Join and finish edges to form an 80-inch length.

With right side of fabric uppermost, pin then zigzag stitch one edge of entredeux over edge of gingham strip, allowing 3/8-inch seam allowance on fabric but stitching close to woven edge of entredeux. Attach remaining edge of entredeux to another gingham strip, and so on, until five gingham strips and four entredeux strips have been joined for quilt top. Trim fabric seam allowances close to zigzagged seams.

With right sides together, stitch white fabric strip across one end of quilt top. Finish remaining long raw edge of white strip with a narrow double hem (see page 127).

With right sides together, stitch the completed quilt top to the white backing, matching raw edges of sides and lower edges, but allowing the top edge of the backing to extend about 14 inches beyond the quilt top, to form overlap. Turn cover right side out. Finish each side edge of overlap with narrow hem.

With right sides together, stitch strip of tiny-checked gingham to upper edge of overlap. Fold this binding strip in half lengthwise, right sides together, and stitch along each side edge. Turn strip right side out and press under 3/8 inch along remaining raw edge. Top-stitch this pressed edge in place over seam, forming a neat binding for upper edge of overlap.

Baste zigzag-edged eyelet lace to folded edge of binding, allowing edge of lace to extend beyond binding, then stitch in place with a narrow zigzag stitch. If you are using a straight eyelet lace with a central zigzag motif, you will need to cut superfluous lace carefully away beyond stitching, leaving a zigzagged edge.

Sew four buttons to the quilt top at the top of each row of entredeux, then work four corresponding buttonholes in the edge of the overlap binding.

Buttoned Pillowcase with Inset Trim

❧ 3/4 yard x 60"-wide light blue
fabric, such as poplin or light chambray
❧ 12" x 25 1/2" white fabric
❧ two strips of blue-and-white-striped or finely
checked fabric, each 3/4" x 25 1/2", for piping
❧ 3/4 yard x 5/8"-wide Swiss embroidery
or eyelet lace, with entredeux edge
❧ five buttons

Finished size: 24" x 28", which fits a large, standard bed pillow, but measurements can be adapted as desired.

Trim light blue fabric to 60" x 25 1/2", and press under 3/8 inch on one short side. Press white fabric in half lengthwise and press under 5/8 inch on the 25 1/2-inch edges.

Fold each striped or checked piping strip in half lengthwise, wrong sides together, and press. On each side of entredeux strip, baste a piping strip, with folded edges towards center, about 3/8 inch apart.

Pin the folded edge of the light blue fabric in place over one piping strip, taking care that the folded edge of the piping extends slightly beyond the blue edge. Top-stitch in place close to the folded edge of light blue fabric, through all thicknesses.

Pin remaining piped edge of entredeux between two pressed edges of white fabric, again taking care that piping remains visible *(see diagram 1)*. Baste and stitch.

DIAGRAM 1

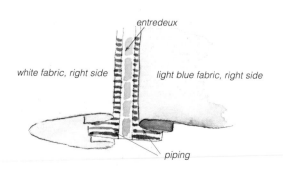

entredeux

white fabric, right side

light blue fabric, right side

piping

Work five buttonholes in doubled white fabric, 1¼ inches in from folded edge and approximately 3½ inches apart.

Finish remaining 25½-inch raw edge of light blue fabric with a narrow machine-stitched hem.

Now fold completed pillowcase piece crosswise, right sides together, and pin so that about 9 inches of light blue fabric extends beyond folded white edge.

Fold this extending fabric back on itself, wrong sides together, thus forming a 9-inch placket (*see diagram 2*).

Stitch sides of pillowcase together, allowing ⅝-inch seams, and finish raw edges of seam allowances.

Turn pillowcase right side out and sew buttons to placket to correspond with buttonholes.

DIAGRAM 2

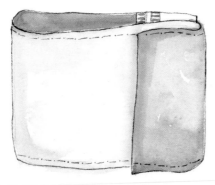

Pillowcase with Zigzag Eyelet Lace Trim

🦢 *3/4 yard x 60"-wide light blue fabric, such as poplin or light chambray*
🦢 *10½" x 25½" white fabric*
🦢 *3/4 yard x 1¼"-wide zigzag-edged eyelet lace*
🦢 *two strips of blue-and-white-striped or finely checked fabric, each 3/4" x 25½", for piping*
🦢 *five buttons*

Finished size: 24" x 28", which fits a large, standard bed pillow, but measurements can be adapted as desired.

Press white fabric in half lengthwise, wrong sides together, and press under ⅝ inch on 25½-inch edges.

Fold each striped or checked piping strip in half lengthwise, wrong sides together, and press.

Baste a piping strip under one pressed edge of white fabric so that fold of piping extends slightly beyond pressed edge. Pin zigzag-edged eyelet lace between two pressed edges of white fabric and top-stitch close to edge, sandwiching eyelet lace and piping together between pressed white edges.

Trim light blue fabric to 60" x 25½", and press under ⅜ inch on one short end.

Baste remaining piping strip under this pressed edge so that piping extends slightly beyond pressed edge, then pin and baste this piped edge onto folded edge of white fabric. Carefully stitch through all layers, close to pressed edge of blue fabric.

Work five buttonholes in doubled white fabric, 1¼ inches in from outside edge and about 3½ inches apart.

Finish remaining short edge of light blue fabric with a narrow machine-stitched hem. Complete pillowcase as for Buttoned Pillowcase with Inset Trim on page 10.

Pillowcase with Ruffles

    ❧ *1¼ yards x 45"-wide blue gingham*
    ❧ *¾ yard x 45"-wide tiny-checked blue gingham*
    ❧ *2 yards x ⅝"-wide Swiss embroidery or eyelet lace,*
        with entredeux edge
    ❧ *4½ yards x 1¼"-wide zigzag-edged eyelet lace*

Finished size: 24" x 28" (excluding ruffles), which fits a large, standard bed pillow, but measurements can be adapted as desired.

From blue gingham, cut two rectangles, each 28½" x 24½", for the front and back, and one 9" x 24½" rectangle for the placket. ⅜-inch seam allowance is included.

From tiny-checked gingham, cut enough 5-inch-wide strips to give 4½ yards total length.

Without cutting it first, pin entredeux to front of pillowcase, about 3 inches in from edges, remembering to allow for, and marking, mitered, or dovetailed, corners. Remove the pins and stitch miters in entredeux following method described in Pillowcase with Lace Edging (*see diagram 1*, on page 8). Trim seam allowances and press them flat. Place entredeux on front of pillowcase again and stitch in place along each edge of entredeux using a narrow zigzag stitch. Press, then carefully cut away gingham from behind entredeux and any excess seam allowance on entredeux itself.

With right sides facing, stitch ends of ruffle strips together, if necessary. With right sides facing, stitch eyelet lace to one long raw edge of ruffle. With right sides facing, stitch short ends of ruffle together, to form a loop.

Run a gathering thread along remaining raw edge of ruffle. Divide ruffle into quarters and mark each quarter with a pin. Draw up gathers to fit around edges of pillowcase front. Pin, then baste ruffle to pillowcase, matching pins with pillowcase corners and easing gathers into the corners to avoid pulling.

Zigzag raw edge of one long side of placket piece, then turn under and stitch a narrow hem. With right sides together and raw edges even, baste placket across one short side of front (*see diagram*).

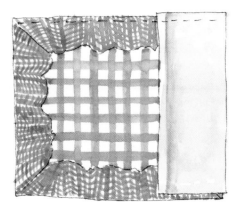

Zigzag raw edge of one short side of pillowcase back, then turn under and stitch a narrow hem (for opening).

With right sides facing, place front and back together, matching hemmed back with placket. Stitch, allowing ⅜-inch seams, sandwiching ruffle and placket at the same time, and taking care not to catch ruffle in seam.

Zigzag seam allowances, zigzag raw edges and turn pillowcase right side out.

PINK QUILT COVER
WITH TIES

❧ 2 1/4 yards x 60"-wide cotton print
❧ 4 1/4 yards x 60"-wide checked fabric
❧ thread

Finished size: Approximately 54" x 79".

From cotton print, cut one 55" x 68" rectangle for the quilt top, and eight 4" x 11" strips for ties.

From checked fabric, cut one 55" x 91" rectangle for back/upper border, two 8" x 59" strips for the ruffle, one 7" x 55" strip for the facing, and one 12" x 55" strip for the flap. 3/8-inch seam allowance is included in all measurements.

Fold each tie in half lengthwise, right sides together, and stitch long edges and across one short end. Trim corners almost to stitching, turn right side out and press.

With right sides together and raw edges even, pin four ties to one short (lower) edge of quilt top, placing the two outer ties approximately 6 inches in from each edge, and positioning remaining two ties evenly between the first two (about 14" apart). Baste ties to hold.

Press under 1/4 inch on one long edge of facing, then press under another 3/8 inch, and stitch hem in place.

With right sides together, stitch facing to lower edge of quilt top, sandwiching ties at the same time. Turn facing to inside and press. Baste raw edges together at sides.

With right sides together and raw edges even, baste remaining four ties in position along one short (lower) edge of quilt back, placing them at the same intervals as previous ties.

Press under 3/8 inch on one long edge of flap, then press under another 3/4 inch and stitch hem in place.

With right sides together, stitch flap to lower edge of quilt back, sandwiching ties at the same time.

With right sides together, stitch ruffle strips together along one short edge and press seam allowances open. Press under 3/8 inch on one long edge of ruffle, then press under another 3/4 inch and stitch hem in place. Run a gathering thread along remaining long raw edge of ruffle and draw up gathers to fit along upper edge of quilt top, distributing fullness evenly.

With *wrong* side of ruffle facing *right* side of quilt top, and raw edges even, stitch ruffle to quilt top. Baste raw edges together at sides.

With right sides together and using ruffle stitching line as a guide, stitch quilt back to quilt top along upper edge.

With quilt top uppermost, and bringing right sides together, fold quilt back around so that lower edges are even *(see diagram 1)*. Pin raw edges together at sides. Fold flap back over quilt top so that right sides of flap and facing are together. Stitch cover at sides, securing raw edges of ruffle at the same time. Fold flap back to quilt back and turn cover right side out.

Insert quilt into cover, tucking end into placket, then knot ties to secure *(see diagram 2)*.

DIAGRAM 1

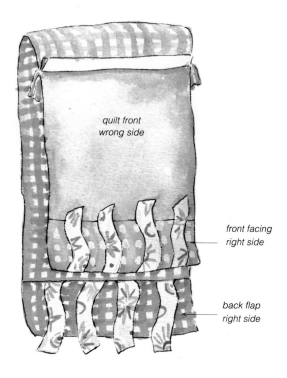

quilt front
wrong side

front facing
right side

back flap
right side

DIAGRAM 2

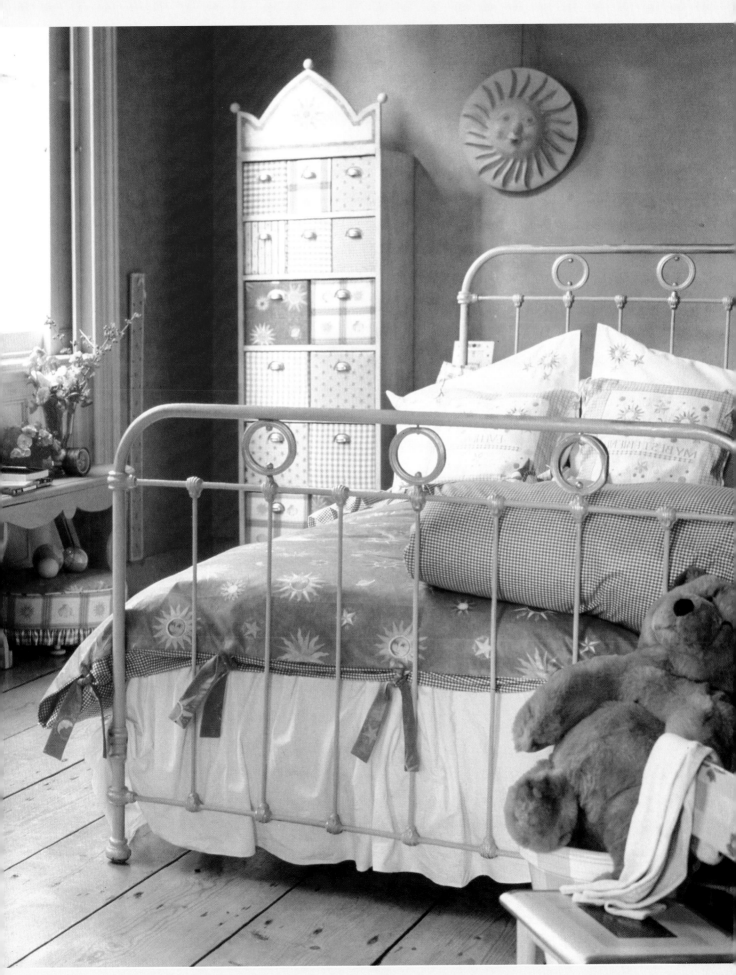

▲ *A plain sheet or pillowcase is enlivened by sewing a contrasting strip of fabric along the top edge or side. The strip can match the pattern of the bedroom curtains or other furnishings in the room, or simply accent the overall color scheme.*
Patterned bed linen can be trimmed in the same way, either with a plain fabric of a different texture (satin on cotton, for example), or with a cheerful print that gives the finished item a richer, more sumptuous appearance.

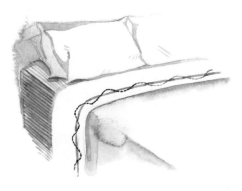

▲ *Ready-made sheets look as though they are custom-made when decorated with a little hand embroidery. A wavy line of running stitch or stem stitch is easily executed by the novice sewer, while those more competent with a needle could try stitches such as feather, fern, chain or satin.*

SHEETS

STENCILED COMFORTER

Brighten up a child's room with hand-stenciled bedcovers. Use primary colors, or choose shades that match the existing decor of the room. A light and dark shade of each color has been used for this comforter and pillowcase to make the paintwork more interesting.

🦋 *white comforter*
🦋 *white pillowcase*
🦋 *sheets of cardboard for stencils*
🦋 *carbon paper (if not photocopying)*
🦋 *craft blade or Xacto knife*
🦋 *waterproof spray paint*
🦋 *fabric paints in light and dark green, light and dark blue, yellow and orange, pink and red*
🦋 *paintbrush*
🦋 *sheet of cardboard, for separating covers*

Note: You can use purchased stencils or make your own. Large stencil cards are available from the stationery sections of office supply stores. However, the smaller stencil cards may be easier to find. The stencils of the alphabet and numerals we used were 2 inches high.

Enlarge small stencil cards on a photocopier, then glue the photocopies onto the cardboard and cut out the letters and numerals using a craft blade. Alternatively, design stencils on graph paper to ensure all letters and numbers are the same height. Using carbon paper, transfer outline to cardboard and cut out.

Spray both sides of each stencil with waterproof paint and leave to dry.

If fabric is new, wash it well in hot, soapy water and rinse to remove sizing. (Fabric paints will not absorb evenly into sized fabric.) Allow fabric to dry, then press it before stenciling. Slip a sheet of cardboard under the area to be stenciled to ensure that the color is confined to only one layer of fabric.

Mix paints to a thick, runny consistency. Practice with a stencil and piece of fabric before attempting the real thing. The best way to handle the brush is to use a dabbing action. Each numeral and letter is painted with two colors – a light and a dark shade.

Using stencil, brush and paint, dab paint onto fabric. Allow stenciling to dry when you can go no further without smudging the work. Add more stenciled motifs after the first are dry. Continue in this manner until both comforter and pillowcase are covered with motifs.

When dry, press the fabric paint at the temperature recommended by the manufacturer.

PILLOWCASES

Pillowcase in One Piece

This is a basic pillowcase pattern from which you can derive more complex looks.

❧ *2/3 yard x 72"-wide fabric* ❧ *thread*

Finished size: Approximately 29" x 19".

Cut a 65½" x 20" fabric piece. ⅜-inch seam allowance is included. Stitch a ⅜-inch hem on one narrow end of fabric piece. Turn under ⅜ inch and then ¾ inch on the other end of fabric, stitch. Bringing right sides together, fold under 29 inches of this end, press. Fold remaining 6 inches of flap over ¾-inch-hemmed edge. Stitch along both sides *(see diagram)*. Trim and zigzag seam allowances. Turn pillowcase right side out; press.

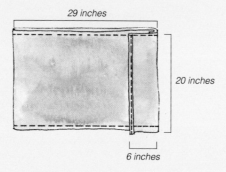

29 inches

20 inches

6 inches

Standard Pillowcase

This pillowcase has a hemmed opening with no flap.

❧ *2/3 yard x 72"-wide fabric* ❧ *thread*

Finished size: Approximately 29" x 19".

Cut a 68" x 20" fabric piece. ⅜-inch seam allowance is included. With right sides together, fold fabric piece in half across its width, stitch along sides. Trim and zigzag seam allowances. Press under ⅜ inch then a 4-inch hem around open edge of pillowcase, stitch *(see diagram)*. Turn pillowcase right side out; press.

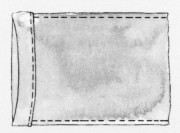

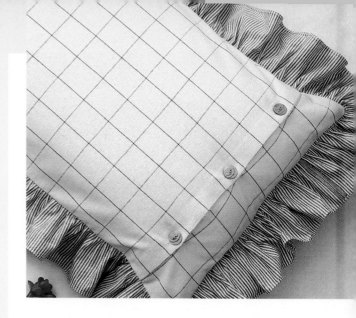

Buttoned Pillowcase with Ruffle

❧ *1¼ yards x 36"-wide fabric*
❧ *2/3 yard x 36"-wide coordinating fabric*
❧ *three buttons* ❧ *thread*

Finished size: Approximately 37" x 27" (including ruffle).

From main fabric, cut one 30" x 20" rectangle for front pillowcase, and one 28" x 20" rectangle and one 8" x 20" rectangle for back pillowcase. From coordinating fabric, cut four strips, each 36" x 5", for ruffle. ⅜-inch seam allowance is included.

Press under ¼ inch along one 20-inch edge of each back section. Press under another 1¾ inches and stitch.

Make three evenly spaced buttonholes along edge of larger back piece. Sew buttons onto smaller back piece to correspond. Button back pieces together.

With right sides together, stitch ruffle strips together at 5-inch edges to form a continuous loop. Stitch a small hem along one raw edge of ruffle. Stitch two rows of gathering on other edge. Pull up gathers to fit pillowcase.

With right sides together and matching raw edges, pin and baste ruffle to front pillowcase. With ruffle facing center of pillowcase, pin back pieces over front, right sides together *(see diagram)*. Baste, stitch and zigzag seam allowances. Turn pillowcase right side out; press.

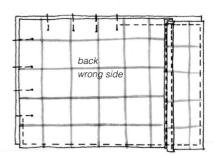

back
wrong side

Pillowcase with Scalloped Edge

- 2 yards x 45"-wide fabric
- small piece of cardboard
- tailor's chalk
- thread

Finished size: Approximately 37" x 27" (including border).

Cut one 30" x 20" piece fabric for front. Cut two 20" x 17" pieces fabric for back. Cut two 38" x 9" fabric strips and two 28" x 9" fabric strips for scalloped borders. 3/8-inch seam allowance is included.

Fold 9-inch-wide strips in half lengthwise, right sides together. From one corner, measure in 4½ inches along long raw edges and mark. Rule a line from mark diagonally out to corner fold, then cut along this line.

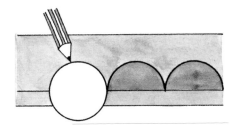

Repeat on each end of each border strip. Unfold strips and press flat. Place a short and long strip together, right sides facing and raw edges even. Stitch pointed ends together, pivoting at point and starting and stopping seam exactly 3/8 inch from each raw edge. Add remaining strips in this manner to form one continuous "frame". With right sides together, press, matching raw edges and miter seams.

Make a scallop-edged template, using a glass to draw four or five scallops on cardboard *(see diagram)*.

Using tailor's chalk, trace scallops around folded edges of border "frame", leaving seam allowance and adjusting a little for even-sized corners. Stitch along traced line and trim close to stitching. Clip into points between each scallop. Turn border right side out, press and baste raw edges together.

With right sides together, raw edges even and matching miter seams to corners, stitch border to front piece.

Press under ¼ inch along one 20-inch edge of each back piece, then press under another ¾ inch and stitch close to inner fold. Overlap back pieces approximately 2 inches to form a 30" x 20" piece, and baste edges together to hold.

With right sides together and scalloped border facing center of pillowcase, pin back to front, then stitch around all edges following border stitching line. Zigzag seam allowances and raw edges. Turn pillowcase right side out and press.

Standard Pillowcase with Ties

> 🐾 *1 yard x 60"-wide fabric*
> 🐾 *thread*

Finished size: 28" x 17½".

Cut one 19" x 57½" fabric piece for the pillowcase. Cut two pieces, each 19" x 8", for the facings, and four pieces, each 17" x 4", for the ties. ⅝-inch seam allowance is included.

Fold one tie in half lengthwise, right sides together. Stitch, leaving one short edge open. Trim seam allowance. Turn right side out, press. Repeat for remaining ties.

On one long edge of facing, turn under ⅝ inch then ⅝ inch again, press and stitch. Repeat for remaining facing.

Pin two ties to each end of pillowcase, right sides together. Place each tie 6½ inches in from side and align raw edges of ties with edge of pillowcase.

With right sides together and raw edges matching, pin and stitch facings to each end of pillowcase, sandwiching ties at the same time.

Fold one facing back to inside, leaving other extended, press. With right sides together and seam lines matching, fold pillowcase in half with folded facing uppermost *(see diagram)*. Flip extended facing down over folded facing, bringing right sides together. Stitch side seams. Zigzag seam allowances. Turn pillowcase right side out and press.

European Pillowcase with Faux Flange

> 🐾 *2 yards x 45"-wide fabric*
> 🐾 *matching sewing thread*
> 🐾 *contrasting sewing thread for flange*

Finished size: 25½"-square inside flange and 30"-square including flange.

Cut one 31" x 31" front pillowcase. Cut two 31" x 22" back pillowcases. ⅝-inch seam allowance is included.

Along one 31-inch edge of back piece, press under ⅝ inch then ⅝ inch again and stitch. Repeat on remaining back piece, but turn under 1¼ inches then 1¼ inches. Overlap the smaller back section over larger (right sides uppermost), adjusting until back measures 31 inches *(see diagram)*. Baste edges together.

31 inches

right side

1¼ inches

With right sides together, stitch front to back around all edges. Trim corners, zigzag seam allowances. Turn right side out and press.

Make a line of machine basting 2¼ inches in from edge all around square. (Measure out 2¼ inches from the machine needle and mark the spot on your machine arm with adhesive tape. Align the edge of the fabric with the edge of the tape.) Using wide, closely spaced zigzag stitch or satin stitch, stitch over the line of machine basting with contrasting thread.

*For the most romantic setting, suspend a sheer canopy of netting
or muslin over a bed dressed in lacy white linen.
Using French seams, stitch lengths of fabric into a tube to give required
width and length (adding 16 inches extra to width and
8 inches extra to length, for draping), leaving front opening below hoop in
one seam. Trim canopy edges above where canopy drapes over hoop so that
they taper to an 8-inch-wide point at ceiling level. Stitch trimmed edges of
canopy together. Hem and gather top edge. Stitch a loop of tape at the top
edge. Hem front opening and lower edge. Attach loop to hook, and drape
canopy over hoop, positioning opening at front.*

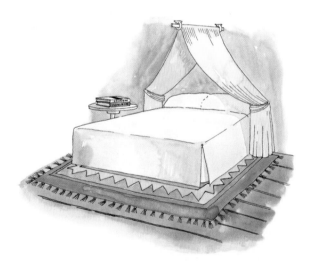

*Replace a traditional headboard with an elegant canopy
to lend a dramatic touch to the bedroom scene.
Fix hooks to ceiling to support pole. Allow enough fabric to drape generously
over the pole and down both sides of the bed. Cut fabric 1 1/2–2 times the pole
length for a gathered canopy, or the same width as pole length.
Hem all edges of fabric, fold in half across width and stitch a casing across
folded edge wide enough to fit pole. Insert pole into casing.
Fix tie-back hooks to wall at either side of bed, swathe a band of fabric
around each end of canopy and attach bands to the hooks.*

CANOPIES

THE CORONA

This simple curtain-plus-canopy adds a stylish touch to a bedroom settings. Make your own curtain or buy it ready-made.

Using a jigsaw, cut a piece of particle-board into a semi-circle 24 inches in diameter. Attach a yard-long flexible curtain rod to the curved edge. Screw two shelf brackets to the underside of the board. Although this construction will be hidden by the curtains, it is a good idea to give the board and brackets a coat of paint. Attach the corona to the wall with the screws provided to fix the brackets, and hang the curtains on the rod.

Insert the last hook on either curtain into the same ring at the center of the rod to ensure that the two panels stay together and completely cover the support board.

Attach a decorative curtain tie-back bracket to the wall on either side of the bed and drape the curtains over the brackets.

PADDED HEADBOARD

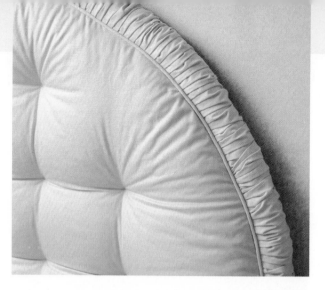

- *sufficient plywood to enable you to cut your headboard (we used particle board)*
- *string and pencil*
- *jigsaw or sharp handsaw*
- *drill*
- *thick polyester batting to cover the front and back (two layers of a thinner batting will do)*
- *fabric for the front and back (amount will depend on size of headboard, but do not forget to allow for the puckering effect of the quilting)*
- *staple gun and staples*
- *long needle, such as a yarn needle*
- *strong linen thread*
- *large, flat buttons for quilting (quantity depends on size of headboard)*
- *fabric for 7-inch-wide edge-strip that measures twice the distance from the base on one side of the headboard, over the top to the base on the other side (you will need to join pieces to make this length)*
- *bias strips of fabric for corded piping, same length, when joined, as ungathered edge-strip*
- *narrow piping cord*

Finished size: These instructions apply to making any sized headboard.

Cut headboard base the desired height and about 2 inches wider than bed. Using string and pencil as a "compass", mark a semi-circle around top of headboard. Cut around this curved line with a jigsaw.

Mark out and drill narrow quilting holes in headboard. The most accurate way to do this is to make a grid of lines of equal distance apart, and drill holes where these lines intersect *(see diagram)*. Our quilting holes are 5 inches apart.

Place polyester batting on one side of the headboard. Smooth it and staple it around the edge of the board about 1 inch in from the edge. Leaving an overhang of about 4 inches around the edge, trim away excess batting.

Place front fabric piece over batting and staple it to the edges of the board, keeping these staples just inside the previous row.

Thread needle with linen thread, take it through a hole, from the back, up through the batting and the fabric, and back down again, having the needle re-enter the fabric about $1/4$ inch away from where it emerged. At the back, pass the ends of the thread through the holes in a button, tying ends firmly into a bow, and pulling the fabric down into the batting. Continue until all quilting is finished.

Run a gathering thread along both long edges of edge-strip, and draw it up until length of strip is equal to the distance around the sides and top of the headboard. Allow a little extra in length for ease.

Make corded piping and apply to both edges of this edge-strip following instructions on page 125. Place one edge of edge-strip against quilted front, with right sides facing and piping stitching level with staples. Staple seam allowance of piping/edge-strip around the headboard in a neat curve, adjusting position of edge-strip until staples clear the other two rows – probably just inside them.

Cover the back of the headboard with another layer of batting and then the back fabric, attaching them in the same manner as front batting and fabric, but omitting any quilting. Bring the remaining edge of the edge-strip over to the back, tuck under the piping seam allowance and baste this, with strong, concealed stitches, to the backing fabric. The excess batting left around the edge becomes padding for the edge-strip.

Tuck under the lower edges of fabric on the bottom of the base towards the back, cutting away any batting likely to cause excess bulk. Hand-sew or staple fabric to neaten the edge.

Stand the headboard behind a studio bed, wedged between the bed and the wall.

CHECKED AND STRIPED CUSHIONS

Seat and Back Cushions for Chair

- *1¹/4 yards x 54"-wide plain fabric*
- *³/4 yard x 54"-wide checked fabric*
- *1¹/4 yards x 54"-wide quilt batting*
- *16-inch zipper*
- *16" x 23" x 2" foam rubber pillow form*
- *polyester fiber fill*

Finished size: Seat cushion 16" x 23"; back cushion 20" x 22". Measure your own furniture and adapt measurements if necessary.

Seat cushion:

From plain fabric, cut a 17" x 24" rectangle, for the top, and two 9¹/2" x 24" rectangles, for the bottom. From the checked fabric, cut two 4¹/2" x 17" strips, and two 4¹/2" x 24" strips, for sides. From batting, cut all parts, as for fabric.

Baste batting shapes to wrong side of appropriate fabric pieces.

Place the two bottom rectangles together, right sides facing, and stitch centre back seam (24-inch edge), allowing a 1-inch seam and leaving an opening of 16 inches in the center for zipper. Insert zipper in opening following instructions on page 126.

With right sides facing, stitch side sections together across short ends, forming one long strip, beginning and ending each seam ³/8 inch from long edge and alternating long and short sections. Stitch remaining short ends together in the same manner, to form a loop.

With right sides together, pin side section to top of cover, matching long and short edges and corner seams, and easing around corners to avoid pulling. Baste, then stitch, allowing a ³/8 inch seam.

Open center back zipper and repeat process for bottom of cover. Turn cover right side out through zipper.

Top-stitch outer edge of cover ⁵/8 inch from finished edge, on both top and bottom, to create a "piping" effect. Stitch as far as possible into the corners, or stitch diagonally across the corners.

Place a layer of batting around foam rubber pillow form, secure with a few basting stitches and insert pillow form into cover.

PILLOWS

Cushions can give a new look to a tired sofa, make a hard chair comfortable and inviting, or provide extra seating. Fabrics can range from durable hand-woven cotton to patterned chintz or delicate lace, and can be imaginatively trimmed with piping, tassels or ruffles. When choosing stuffings, keep in mind the final use of the cushion. Feather stuffing is expensive, but makes soft, supportive pillows that retain their shape. A combination of feather and foam gives a less expensive but comfortable stuffing. Foam chips are cheap but tend to be lumpy and crumble over time. A foam rubber block can be cut to fit a box-style cushion and holds its shape well, while polyester fiber fill is a fully washable, soft stuffing that will compact over time.

Back cushion:

From both fabrics, cut a 21" x 23" rectangle, checked for front and plain for back. From batting, cut two 21" x 23" pieces. From plain fabric, cut four 3" x 7" strips for ties.

Baste a batting piece to wrong side of front and back.

Fold ties in half lengthwise, right sides together, and stitch long edges and across one short end, allowing 3/8-inch seams. Trim corners, turn ties right side out and press. With right sides together and raw edges even, baste ties to both long edges of the cushion front, placing two ties

approximately 2 inches from the top edge, and the remaining two ties approximately 7 inches from the lower edge.

With right sides facing and allowing a 3/8 seam, stitch front and back together around edges, sandwiching ties at the same time, and leaving approximately 6 inches open in one short edge, for turning.

Turn cover right side out, and top-stitch 5/8 inch from finished edge, as for seat cushion, but do not stitch across opening. Fill cushion lightly with polyester fiber fill and slip-stitch opening closed. Complete top-stitching, 5/8 inch from finished edge.

Seat Cushions for Garden Bench

For two seat cushions:
- *1 yard x 54"-wide checked fabric*
- *2 yards x 54"-wide striped fabric*
- *1 yard quilt batting*
- *approximately four skeins six-stranded cotton embroidery floss, for tufting*
- *two foam rubber pillow forms, each 19" x 31" x 3"*
- *long needle and strong thread*

Finished size: Seat cushion measures approximately 21" x 33" x 3" high.

For each cushion:

From checked fabric, cut one 22" x 34" rectangle, for top. From striped fabric, cut one 22" x 34" rectangle, for bottom; plus two 5" x 22" strips, one 5" x 34" strip, and two 3" x 34" strips, for the side sections. From batting, cut two 22" x 34" rectangles.

Baste the batting pieces to the wrong side of top and bottom pieces.

With right sides together and allowing a ½-inch seam, stitch 3" x 34" side strips together along one long edge, leaving a 24-inch opening in center of seam for stuffing. Press seam allowances open, baste open edges together to hold.

With right sides together and ⅜-inch seams, stitch side sections together across short ends, forming one long strip, beginning and ending each seam ⅜ inch from long edge and alternating long and short sections. Stitch remaining short ends together in the same manner, to form a loop.

With right sides together, pin side section to top of cover, matching long and short edges and corner seams, and easing carefully around corners to avoid pulling. Baste, then stitch, allowing a ⅜-inch seam. Repeat process for bottom of cover. Remove basting from opening and turn cover right side out.

Top-stitch outer edge of cover ⅝ inch from finished edge, on both top and bottom, to create a "piping" effect. Stitch as far as possible into the corners, or stitch diagonally across the corners.

Place a layer of batting around pillow form, secure with a few basting stitches and insert pillow form into cover. Slip-stitch back opening closed.

When cushions are complete, make 12 tassels, 1 inch long, from embroidery floss following instructions for Basic Tassels on page 120 and using approximately one-third of a skein per tassel. Using a long needle and strong thread, stitch tassels to cushion *(see diagram)*. Beginning on bottom of cushion, take needle through all layers and out through top. Take needle through the loops on the neck of a tassel, then reinsert needle back through cushion to bottom, pull slightly, take a couple of stitches back and forth, and fasten off very securely. Bury ends of threads in cushion. Place two rows of three tassels, each row approximately 6 inches in from the long edge, and allowing about 9 inches between tassels (six tassels per cushion).

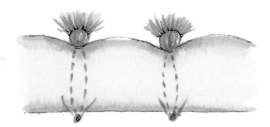

Press under ½ inch on long edge of each back piece, then press under another 2 inches and stitch hem. Work three evenly spaced buttonholes in one hem, the outer ones approximately 6 inches from raw edges. Lap two hemmed pieces over each other (buttonholes on top) so that lapped rectangles match front. Top-stitch along hemline from raw edge towards center for about 3 inches from each end. Sew on covered buttons to correspond with buttonholes.

Cut the fringed edging into two equal pieces and finish raw ends so that each piece measures 22 inches long. With right sides together, stitch fringed edging to each short end of cushion front, matching edges.

With right sides together, stitch front to back around all edges, allowing a ⅜-inch seam and stitching precisely over previous stitching on side edges. Turn cover right side out through button opening. Insert pillow form into cover.

Pillow with Striped Border

- 🐑 *½ yard x 54"-wide checked fabric*
- 🐑 *¾ yard x 54"-wide striped fabric*
- 🐑 *two buttons*
- 🐑 *20-inch-square pillow form*

Pillow with Fringed Edging

- 🐑 *⅔ yard x 54"-wide checked fabric*
- 🐑 *⅔ yard x 54"-wide solid-colored fabric*
- 🐑 *1⅓ yards x 1½"-wide fringed cotton edging*
- 🐑 *five buttons* 🐑 *fiber fill*
- 🐑 *22" x 28" pillow form*

Finished size: Approximately 22" x 28".

From checked fabric, cut one 23" x 29" rectangle, for the front. From solid-colored fabric, cut two 23" x 18" rectangles, for the back.

From scraps of matching fabric, cut circles ¾ inch larger than buttons. Run gathering threads around edges of circles. Place small amount of fiber fill in center of each circle and position button on top. Draw up gathering threads and tie off ends *(see diagram)*.

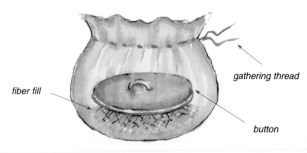

fiber fill

gathering thread

button

Finished size: 20"-square.

Mark a 20-inch square onto paper, then mark a second 12-inch square in the center of this (the inner square has a 4-inch border all round). Cut parts out so that you have a square and a frame.

From checked fabric, cut one square for pillow front, remembering to add 3/8-inch seam allowance all round. From striped fabric, cut one frame, adding 3/8-inch seam allowance to both inner and outer edges. Center fabric on pattern so that stripes run evenly. Cut two 12½" x 21" rectangles, for cushion back.

With right sides together and allowing 3/8-inch seams, stitch outer edges of checked square to inner edges of striped frame, one edge at a time. Cut diagonally in as far as stitching in the corners of the frame so that the finished piece will lie flat.

Press under ½ inch on one long edge of each back piece, then press under another 1 inch and stitch hem. Work two buttonholes in one hem, each approximately 2½ inches from the center. Lap the two hemmed pieces over one another (buttonholes on top) so that they form a 21-inch square, then top-stitch along hemline from raw edge towards center for about 4 inches from each end.

With right sides together and allowing 3/8-inch seams, stitch front to back around outer edges. Clip corners, turn cover right side out. Sew on buttons and insert pillow form.

Floor Cushions

For two floor cushions:
❧ *1 yard x 54"-wide checked fabric*
❧ *1 yard x 54"-wide contrast checked fabric*
❧ *two foam rubber pillow forms,*
each 21" x 30" x 3"
❧ *1¼ yards x 54"-wide quilt batting*

Finished size: Approximately 22" x 31".

From checked fabric, cut one 26" x 35" rectangle, for front. From contrast check, cut one 26" x 35" rectangle, for back.

Before stitching, place pins on either side of each corner, 2¼ inches from corner, on both front and back, to mark pleats. With right sides together, fold each piece diagonally from the corner so that the pin markers meet. Working at right angle to the raw edge, work a 1-inch line of stitching, 2¼ inches from corner, to create a corner pleat. Press pleat well. Repeat for remaining corners on front and back.

With right sides together and allowing a 3/8-inch seam, stitch front to back, leaving an opening in one seam for turning and pillow form insertion. Trim all corners diagonally and turn cover right side out.

Cover pillow form with layer of batting, baste to hold. Insert pillow form into cover, slip-stitch opening closed.

DAYBED COVER AND ACCESSORIES

Daybed Cover

🐦 *fabric (we used ticking)*
🐦 *piping cord*
🐦 *thread*
🐦 *zipper (length of one long side of daybed)*

Measure the length and width of the mattress and add ⅝-inch seam allowance on all edges, for top and bottom cover pieces. Measure depth and perimeter of mattress and add ⅝-inch seam allowance on all edges, for side piece.

Cut one fabric piece for top cover and one for bottom cover. Trim each corner of cover pieces into a curve. Cut and join fabric strips for side piece.

Piping will be stitched around four edges of top cover piece, and around three edges (two short edges and one long edge) of bottom cover piece. Measure around cover pieces and make required amount of corded piping following instructions on page 125. Apply piping to top and bottom cover pieces, continuing piping around the corners of the unpiped edge of bottom cover piece.

With right sides facing, stitch ends of side piece together to give a continuous loop. Zigzag raw edges. With right sides together, pin and stitch one edge of side piece around three piped edges of bottom cover piece. Insert zipper between edge of side piece and unpiped edge of bottom cover following instructions on page 126. Open zipper.

Pin and stitch remaining edge of side piece to top cover piece. Clip seam allowances at corners and zigzag raw edges. Turn right side out, insert mattress and close zipper.

Valance

🐦 *fabric (we used ticking)*
🐦 *thread*

Measure the width and length of daybead base and add ⅝-inch seam allowance on all edges, for base panel. Measure the perimeter of daybed base, double the measurement and add ⅝-inch seam allowance, for ruffled skirt. (If desired, skirt may be made to fit around three sides of daybed rather than four.) Measure from daybed base to desired depth and add ⅝-inch seam allowance on all edges, for skirt depth.

Cut one fabric piece for base panel, then trim each corner into a curve. Cut fabric strips for skirt.

Join fabric strips for skirt, then join ends of skirt to give a continuous loop. Trim and stitch a narrow hem on one long edge of skirt.

Stitch two rows of gathering along other edge of skirt. Pull up gathers to fit around base panel. With right sides together, pin skirt around base panel, concentrating extra gathers at each corner. Stitch, zigzag raw edges and place valance over daybed base.

Square Pillow

🐦 *⅔ yard x 60"-wide fabric*
🐦 *22-inch-square pillow form*
🐦 *thread*

Finished size: Approximately 22"-square.

Cut front and back cushion pieces, each 23 inches square. Cut a 40" x 5" strip for bow. ⅜-inch seam allowance is included.

Pin front to back, right sides together, stitch all around leaving a 14-inch opening on one side. Trim raw edges, turn right side out, press. Fill with pillow form, slip-stitch opening closed.

Fold bow strip in half lengthwise, right sides together. Trim ends diagonally. Stitch along raw edges, leaving a small opening in center on long edge. Turn right side out, slip-stitch opening closed, press. Tie into a bow and sew onto pillow front.

Plain Neckroll Pillow

- 1 yard x 45"-wide fabric
- 16-inch zipper
- 1³/4 yards piping cord

- 1 yard x 45"-wide fabric, for pillow form
- polyester fiber fill • thread

Finished size: Approximately 24" x 8".

Cut one 27" x 25" piece for pillow. Cut two 9½-inch-diameter circles for ends. ⅝-inch seam allowance is included. Cut enough 1½-inch-wide bias strips to equal at least twice the circumference of the end circles, when joined.

Make and apply corded piping around edge of each end piece following instructions on page 125. Stitch 27" edges of pillow piece together, leaving 16-inch opening in seam center for zipper. Zigzag raw edges and press seam allowances open, turn pillow right side out. Insert zipper following instructions on page 126. Open zipper, turn pillow wrong side out.

Pin ends to pillow, right sides together, placing pins next to stitching line. Stitch, zigzag raw edges, turn pillow right side out.

Cut and make pillow form in same way as neckroll pillow, omitting piping and zipper. Turn pillow form right side out, stuff with fiber fill and slip-stitch opening closed. Place pillow form into cover and close zipper.

BUTTONED ROUND PILLOW

- 🖝 1¼ yards x 45"-wide fabric
- 🖝 2¾ yards purchased bias-binding for piping, or make your own following instructions on page 125
- 🖝 2¾ yards narrow piping cord
- 🖝 polyester fiber fill
- 🖝 two buttons
- 🖝 quilting thread
- 🖝 doll needle
- 🖝 thread

Finished size: 14" diameter.

Cut pillow pattern using a 15-inch square of paper. Fold paper into quarters. Pin one end of a piece of string to center of paper, tie a pencil onto other end of string 7½ inches from pin. Draw a quarter circle with a 7½ inch radius *(see diagram 1)*.

Cut two circles of fabric using pattern. Cut one 45" x 3" strip for pillow side. Measurements include ⅜-inch seam allowance.

Using purchased or self-fabric bias, make 2¾ yards corded piping and apply to edges of cushion front and back (see instructions on page 125.)

DIAGRAM 1

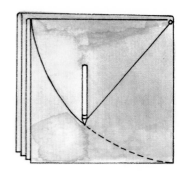

With right sides facing, stitch 3-inch edges of pillow side together. Trim and press open seam allowances, and finish raw edges.

With right sides together and raw edges even, pin one edge of side piece to pillow front over piping. Machine stitch using zipper foot.

Pin other edge of side piece to pillow back, right sides together and raw edges even, leaving an opening in one side for stuffing fiber fill. Turn cover right side out, insert fiber fill and slip-stitch opening closed.

Use scraps of fabric to cover buttons following method described in Pillow with Fringed Edging on page 30.

Use quilting thread and a large needle to sew a few stitches through the center of the pillow, stitching through all layers and pulling thread taut *(see diagram 2)*. Sew a button in center of front and back of pillow over stitches.

DIAGRAM 2

PILLOW WITH TWISTED CORD PIPING OR FRINGE

🐦 *1/2 yard x 45"-wide fabric*

🐦 *1 3/4 yards twisted cord piping or fringe, with a flange for insertion*

🐦 *14-inch zipper*

🐦 *thread*

Finished size: To fit a 16"-square pillow form.

Cut one 17-inch square for pillow front and one 17" x 17 3/8" piece for pillow back. 3/8-inch seam allowance is included. Use a glass to curve corners.

Pin flange of piping or fringe to right side of front pillow, starting at center of one edge and aligning edge of flange with raw edge of fabric. Using a zipper foot, stitch around all sides, overlapping ends and trimming excess to finish *(see diagram 1)*. Clip flange on the corners, but take care not to cut piping or it will unravel.

DIAGRAM 1

Pin pillow front to back, right sides together. Stitch, leaving 3/4-inch seam allowance along bottom (zipper) edge of back piece. Leave central opening for zipper in this seam.

Open zipper and, with wrong side of pillow back uppermost, place zipper tape face down on piping seam allowance of pillow front so that tape edge is approximately 1/4 inch in from raw edge *(see diagram 2)*. Pin then baste along center of tape on piping stitching line. Stitch, following basted seamline.

Turn pillow right side out. Close zipper. Press under 3/4-inch on back

DIAGRAM 2

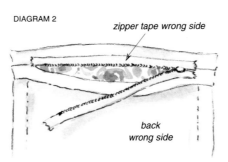

zipper tape wrong side

back wrong side

DIAGRAM 3

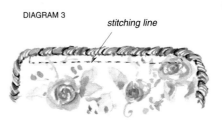

stitching line

piece zipper edge so that fold abuts the edge of piping. Pin then baste folded edge to zipper from the right side, close to zipper teeth, then stitch in position, stitching across both ends of zipper as far as the piping *(see diagram 3)*.

Remove all basting and place the pillow form inside cover.

TASSELED NECKROLL PILLOW

- *3/4 yard x 45"-wide gold satin*
- *1/4 yard x 45"-wide embroidered organza (see **Note**)*
- *3/4 yard x 2 1/2"-wide decorative flat braid*
- *1 1/4 yards x 1/4"-diameter gold flanged twisted satin cord*
- *1 1/4 yards x 3/8"-diameter gold flanged twisted satin cord*
- *1 2/3 yards crochet cotton or heavy cotton*
- *45" x 50" thin batting*
- *small piece cardboard*
- *craft blade or Xacto knife*
- *two skeins six-strand cotton embroidery floss (burgundy)*
- *silk embroidery thread: one skein each pale gold and burgundy*
- *assorted beads in gold and burgundy, for tassels*
- *two 1-inch-diameter gold buttons, with shanks*
- *embroidery needle*
- *beading needle*
- *craft glue*
- *thread*

Finished size: Approximately 14" long; 7" diameter.

Note: We mounted a remnant of embroidered bridal organza over the top of the gold satin for the main body of the pillow, but this is not strictly necessary – a single fabric, such as the satin alone, will do as well. If you are using a decorative fabric, remember to allow for the nap; obvious patterns should run around the pillow, not across it.

From gold satin, cut one 15" x 21" rectangle for the pillow body. Cut two rectangles on the bias, each 5" x 21", for the pillow ends, and two circles, each with diameter of 6". From organza (if you are using it), cut one 15" x 21" rectangle.

Place organza rectangle on top of satin pillow body and baste layers together around all edges. Center braid along length of pillow body and tuck flange of 1/4-inch satin cord under braid on each side. Baste to hold, then stitch, securing braid and cord in one operation.

With right sides together and allowing a 5/8-inch seam allowance, stitch the short edges of the pillow body together, matching ends of braid and forming a tube.

Pin and stitch flange of 3/8-inch satin cord along seamline on each end of tube, overlapping cord ends in seam allowance to finish. With right sides together, stitch the short edges of bias tubes. Press under 1/4 inch, then another 3/8 inch on one edge of both tubes and stitch close to inner edge to form a casing, leaving about 5/8 inch open through which to insert the crochet cotton.

With right sides together, and matching raw edges and center back seams, pin and stitch pillow ends to pillow body, stitching on original piping stitchline. Carefully ease bias-cut pillow ends, as they will tend to stretch. Thread crochet cotton through both casings.

Fold batting into thirds, roll up along the width and slip-stitch to secure, forming a cylindrical insert. Place batting into pillow cover.

Overcast raw edges of satin pillow ends, and place over ends of batting, securing around edges with a few basting stitches. Pull crochet cotton up tightly to gather in pillow ends. Tie off ends, tucking excess length inside pillow. (Do not cut it off, or you will need to re-thread casing every time you undo the cover.)

Cut two circles from cardboard, each approximately 1 1/2 inches in diameter. With a craft knife, cut a small circle (approximately 1/4 inch in

diameter) in the center of each circle. Using three strands of burgundy embroidery floss, work tightly packed buttonhole stitch around circle *(see diagram 1 and general instructions on page 126)*, adding new lengths of thread as needed by joining at the back. If desired, some sections can be worked in pale gold silk thread.

DIAGRAM 1

Using pale gold and burgundy silk thread (half a skein of each in each tassel), make two simple 2½-inch long tassels (see Basic Tassels on page 120). Tie strands at top of tassels with only two strands of embroidery floss, 8 inches long, as they need to pass through the beads. Thread tassel ties through decorative beads using a beading needle. Attach one tassel to each covered circle, securing at back *(see diagram 2)*.

DIAGRAM 2

Using a little craft glue, secure a gold button to each covered circle so that button shank protrudes through center hole. Reaching through casing opening, stitch button shank to satin circle in center of each pillow end.

ROUND CUSHION WITH RUFFLE AND PIPING

- 1¼ yards x 45"-wide fabric
- 3 yards purchased bias binding for piping, or make your own following instructions on page 125
- 3 yards narrow piping cord
- 16-inch-diameter pillow form
- 12-inch zipper
- thread

Finished size: Approximately 21" diameter, including ruffle.

Cut one 16½-inch-diameter circular cushion pattern, measuring an 8¼-inch radius and following method described in Buttoned Round Cushion on page 34. ⅜-inch seam allowance is included.

Cut cushion front using this pattern piece. Fold pattern in half and add ¾ inch along straight edge to make back pattern. Cut two backs.

Cut a 6½-inch-wide ruffle strip about twice the length of cushion circumference. (Our strip for a 16 inch-diameter cushion was 100 inches long.)

Stitch ruffle strip ends together, right sides facing, to form a loop, and press seam allowances open. Fold ruffle in half lengthwise, wrong sides together, to make a double fabric ruffle, press. Fold ruffle into quarters, mark quarters with pins at raw edge.

Stitch a row of gathering from one pin to the next, leaving a long thread at each pin. Make a second row of gathering stitches in the same way.

Using bias strips, make corded piping and apply to cushion front following instructions on page 125.

Fold front into quarters and mark with pins. Pull up gathers on ruffle, matching each "pin to pin" length to each front quarter. Tie threads in a figure-eight around each pin to hold gathers in place.

Pin ruffle onto cushion front over piping, placing pins on wrong side of cushion front along stitching line. Baste, then stitch, using zipper foot.

Press under ¾ inch on straight edge of each back piece. Zigzag raw edges and insert zipper following instructions on page 126. Open zipper.

With right sides together and raw edges even, pin front to back. Stitch, trim seam allowances and zigzag raw edges. Turn right side out, press.

Place pillow form inside cover.

folded edges onto right side of piped cushion piece, at marked position, so that it is equal with raw edges (*see diagram*). Using zipper foot, stitch across ties through all thicknesses, following piping stitching line.

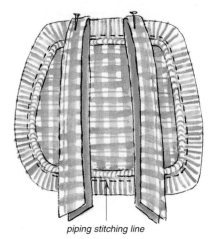

piping stitching line

TIE-ON RUFFLED CHAIR CUSHION

- *1 yard x 45"-wide main fabric, for front, back and ties (depending on size of chair seat)*
- *2/3 yard x 45"-wide first contrast fabric, for ruffle*
- *1/3 yard x 45"-wide second contrast fabric, for piping (see **Note**, below)*
- *2 yards piping cord (pre-shrink it by dipping it into hot water and squeezing dry)*
- *thread*
- *7-8 ounces polyester fiber fill*

Finished size: 17" x 18" (excluding ruffle), or to fit your chair.

Note: Fabric quantities given are for the chair cushion pictured; you may need a little more or less depending on the size of your chair seat. If you wish to make your piping from the main fabric, you will need an extra 4 inches of fabric instead of a second contrast.

Cut cushion pattern to fit chair. Place sheet of paper on chair seat and trace outline. Add on approximately 1½ inches around outline to allow for thickness of cushion and ⅝ inch seam allowance. Use a dinner plate to curve the corners.

From main fabric, cut cushion front and back, and two 45" x 8" strips for ties (cut across fabric, from selvage to selvage).

From first contrast fabric, cut enough 8-inch-wide strips across fabric from selvage to selvage to equal, when joined, about twice the outer edge measurement of the cushion.

From second contrast fabric, cut enough 1½-inch-wide bias strips to equal, when joined, the outer edge measurement of the cushion.

Mark tie positions and quilting points on cushion front and back.

Following instructions on page 125, join bias strips and make necessary length of corded piping. Starting at one back corner, apply piping to all edges of one cushion piece.

Fold tie strips in half lengthwise, right side together, then cut ends of both pieces at an angle. Stitch along all raw edges, leaving an opening in center of long edge. Turn ties right side out, pulling pointed corners out neatly, then slip-stitch the openings closed, and press.

Fold ties in half crosswise, having angled ends even. Pin each of the folded edges onto right side of piped cushion piece, at marked position, so that it is equal with raw edges.

Pin tie ends to center of trimmed cushion piece to keep them out of the way of further stitching.

Join ruffle strips to create length measuring about twice the outer edge of cushion, then join short ends to form a circle. Fold circle of fabric in half lengthwise, wrong sides together and raw edges even. Press, then run two rows of gathering along raw edges. Draw up to create gathers.

With raw edges even and right sides facing, pin ruffle around piped cushion piece, pinning from unpiped side through the previous stitching. Using zipper foot, stitch ruffle in place following previous stitching.

With right sides facing and raw edges even, pin then stitch remaining cushion piece to trimmed piece, leaving a 6-inch opening at center back for stuffing. Turn cushion to right side and remove pins holding ties.

Pin through both thicknesses at quilting points, then stitch a small square around each, three times.

Place filling into cushion, starting at front and working back to opening, creating a firm, evenly stuffed cushion. Slip-stitch opening closed.

PIPED SQUARE PILLOW

- *3/4 yard x 54"-wide fabric, or 1 1/4 yards x 45"-wide fabric*
- *2 1/3 yards purchased bias binding for corded piping, or make your own following instructions on page 125*
- *2 1/3 yards piping cord*
- *19-inch-square pillow form*
- *three buttons*
- *thread*

Finished size: 19" square.

Cut one 20-inch-square piece for front. Cut one 20" x 19" piece for upper back and one 20" x 8 1/2" piece for lower back. 3/8-inch seam allowance is included in measurements.

Press under 2 1/2 inches along one 20" edge of each back piece to form self facing. Zigzag raw edge of each facing.

Make three evenly spaced buttonholes along folded edge of upper back piece, with the outer buttonholes approximately 4 inches from the pillow edge.

Sew buttons onto lower back piece to correspond with buttonholes, then button back pieces together (back should now be same size as front), and stitch across top and bottom of folded edges.

Using purchased or self-fabric bias, make corded piping and apply to all edges of front piece following instructions on page 125.

With right sides together, pin then baste back piece to front piece over piping. Stitch, using zipper foot and following piping stitching line. Trim corners and seam allowances, zigzag raw edges.

Turn cover right side out; press. Place pillow form in cover.

PIPED CHAIR CUSHION

- ❧ 1½ yards x 45"-wide fabric
- ❧ 3 yards narrow piping cord
- ❧ 2-inch-thick foam, cut to size
- ❧ thread

Finished size: 16-inch diameter, or to fit your chair.

Make pattern for cushion following method described for Buttoned Round Pillow on page 34, adding ⅜-inch seam allowance all around. Our pattern was 17 inches in diameter (8½-inch radius), including seam allowance.

From fabric, cut cushion top using this pattern. Fold pattern in half and add ¾ inch along straight edge to make back pattern. Cut two backs. Cut two 27" x 3" pieces for gusset (add extra length for larger cushion). Cut four 33" x 5" pieces for ties. Cut enough 1½-inch-wide bias strips to equal twice the length of the circumference of the cushion, when joined. ⅜-inch seam allowance is included in measurements.

Stitch two tie pieces together at 5-inch ends, right sides facing. Fold strip in half lengthwise, right sides together, trim ends diagonally. Stitch along raw edges, leaving small opening in center of long edge. Trim seam allowances, zigzag raw edges, turn right side out and slip-stitch opening closed. Repeat for other tie pieces.

Fold under ¾ inch along straight edge of each bottom piece to form self facing, zigzag raw edges. Overlap pieces to fit top piece, pin together.

Join bias strips, then make and apply corded piping to top and bottom following instructions on page 125.

With right sides facing, stitch ends of gusset pieces together to make a loop. Stitch one edge of gusset to back cushion piece, over piping, right sides and raw edges together. Trim seam allowances, zigzag seams. Repeat to attach gusset to top piece.

Press ties in half across width, angled ends even. Position foldline at back of cushion in positions to match chair, pin to gusset (our ties were 9 inches apart). Hand-sew in place, stitching along foldlines *(see diagram)*.

Insert foam filling and slip-stitch back overlap closed.

CHILD'S BEANBAG

- *2¹/₂ yards x 54"-wide polished cotton upholstery fabric with nap or one-way design, or 1³/₄ yards x 54"-wide polished cotton upholstery fabric without nap*
- *20-inch coordinating zipper*
- *polyester thread*
- *1-pound bag of styrofoam "peanuts"*
- *pliers*

Finished size: Approximately 42" from tip to base; 20" base diameter.

Following grid, enlarge pattern pieces onto paper. ⁵/₈-inch seam allowance is included on all pieces except on zipper edges of the base, where ³/₄-inch allowance is included.

If fabric has one-way pattern or nap, place pattern pieces in same direction when laying out on fabric. If fabric is printed, make sure print will be right way up on completed beanbag. Cut three bag segments, label them A, B and C. Trim C only along curved line, as indicated on pattern. Cut two bases.

Join A to B, right sides together, along one long side. Edge-finish or zigzag seam allowances for strength. Press to one side.

Pin C to A/B, starting at base and easing at the top if necessary. Stitch, finish seam allowances.

With right sides together, machine baste straight edges of base sections leaving ³/₄-inch seam allowance. Insert zipper following instructions on page 126. Before removing the basting, stitch around zipper again, ¹/₄ inch away from original stitching, for added strength.

cutting line for C

3/4-inch zipper seam

BASE

SEGMENT –
HALF PATTERN

when cutting pattern, place this edge on fold of paper in order to make full pattern piece

With right sides together, pin base to beanbag body, but avoid matching zipper seam with body seam. Open zipper a little to allow for turning. Clip curves on base of stiffer fabrics. Stitch, zigzag raw edges, turn right side out.

Fill beanbag with about 90 per cent of peanuts, reserving the remainder for refills. Close zipper and, for child safety, use pliers to remove zipper tab. For extra safety, hand-sew over tab to conceal it completely. Re-open zipper with paper clip when necessary.

Scale: 3/4 inch = 4 inches

TAILORED LOOSE COVER FOR SOFA

❧ fabric
❧ piping cord
❧ hooks and eyes, or hook and loop tape
❧ thread
❧ tailor's chalk

Note: Each section of the loose cover is cut out in a rectangle roughly the right size. These pieces are pinned onto the sofa, trimmed and pleated to fit exactly. They are then removed and stitched together, with piping added where necessary.

Measuring

Remove seat cushions and carefully measure each section of the sofa, measuring at the longest and widest points *(see diagram 1)*. Inside arm should be measured from seat over arm to outside of arm, finishing either underneath scroll or halfway around scroll; use original upholstery lines as a guide.

Record the shape and measurement of each piece, then add ⅝-inch seam allowance on all sides and a 6-inch tuck-in allowance, if necessary. Tuck-in allowance should be added where fabric tucks into seat or under cushions; for example, at lower edge of inside arm, lower edge of inside back, and at edges between inside arm and inside back.

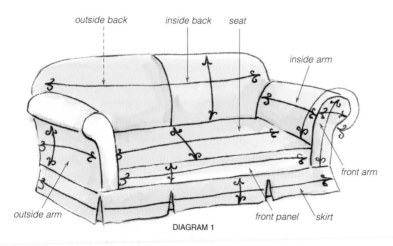

outside back   inside back   seat

inside arm

front arm

outside arm   front panel   skirt

DIAGRAM 1

FURNITURE COVERS

Complicated upholstery is an art best left to professionals, but simple projects, such as re-covering an upholstered seat, can easily be done at home – you will save money and give a new lease on life to tired-looking furniture. We show you how a director's chair becomes ready for dining-room duty in a slipcover, and a dull chair is dressed up for display in under an hour. With a little more time and effort, loose sofa covers will reward, making the luxury of seasonal covers affordable.

Calculate and record skirt measurements, adding 4-inch allowance for kick pleats at each corner of sofa. Also allow 4-inch-wide inserts, same depth as skirt, for kick pleats at corners. If a gathered skirt or no skirt is required, see page 48.

Calculating fabric requirements

Draw a plan, marking in each separate piece and positioning it along the correct grain (see diagram 2). Pieces that are wider than fabric width need to be pieced and the fabric pattern should be matched. In some areas, such as the inside back, it may not be possible to match the pattern; the seam joining the pieces can be piped.

Add together measurements for each piece and calculate fabric requirements. Add extra fabric for piping and cushions. Allow extra fabric for pattern matching.

DIAGRAM 2

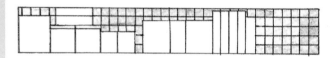

Cutting fabric

Place each pattern piece on the correct grain and, matching fabric pattern wherever possible, cut it out in fabric. Fabric motifs should be placed in the center of each section. Pin an identifying label on each piece. Calculate and make required amount of piping following instructions on page 125.

Pin fitting

Mark center of each section of the sofa and each fabric piece with chalk. Begin pinning fabric pieces to sofa. Pieces can be pinned wrong side out, which makes stitching easier, or right side out if pattern placement needs to be checked (repinning will have to be done before stitching if pieces are pinned right side out).

Pin outside back piece to sofa, keeping crosswise grain parallel to floor and matching centers of sofa and fabric piece. Mark stitching line on fabric with chalk, pin inside back to sofa, then pin pieces together at adjoining seamlines.

Smooth out fabric and check size. Trim fabric to sofa shape, leaving seam allowance and tuck-in allowance intact (see diagram 3).

Continue with inside arm and outside arm sections.

On scroll-armed sofas, trim tuck-in allowance between inside back and inside arm sections so that full 6-inch allowance on lower edge tapers to ⅝-inch seam allowance at top edge (see diagram 4).

DIAGRAM 3

DIAGRAM 4

Both outside back/outside arm seams should be left open to enable cover to be removed. Clip seam allowance around curves.

Pin the seat piece in position between the inside arms and back. For a pull-out sofa bed, the seat piece can be joined with hook and loop tape instead of stitching, to allow bed to unfold.

Pin the front arm pieces next. On a scroll-armed sofa there will be fullness on the inside arm piece that needs to be pleated to fit the front arm piece. Position pleats evenly around arm, pin in place (see diagram 5).

Stitching

Remove cover, apply piping to piped seamlines (see instructions for applying piping on page 125). Stitch main pieces together.

If sofa is box-shaped and has an extra strip between each main section, pin these strips in place as you work.

Place cover on sofa, check fit. Remove cover, make any necessary adjustments, and zigzag raw edges. Pin and stitch front panel in place.

Cut a facing strip 2 inches wide and twice as long as opening between outside back and outside arm. Stitch facing around opening (see diagram 6). Zigzag raw edge of facing and turn to inside of cover.

DIAGRAM 5

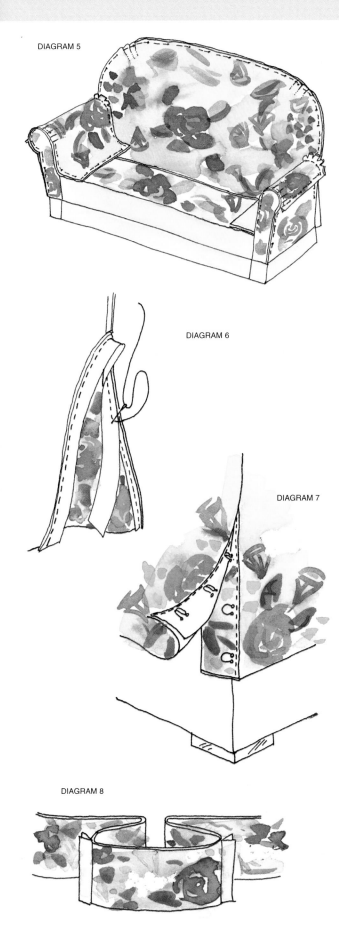

DIAGRAM 6

DIAGRAM 7

DIAGRAM 8

Attach hooks and eyes or hook and loop tape to facing *(see diagram 7)*, positioning fastenings so that edges of outside back and outside arm align.

Stitch pleat insert between each skirt width. Fold each insert into pleat *(see diagram 8)*, baste in place. Stitch piping around lower edge of sofa cover if desired. Stitch skirt in place over piping. Hem lower edge and ends of skirt.

Make covers for seat cushions, using original covers as guides. Apply piping to top and bottom edges.

corner pleat. Allow 4-inch inserts for corner kick pleats, same depth as skirt. Cut out panels and pleat inserts.

Stitch pleat insert between each skirt panel, fold into pleat, baste in place along upper edge. Fold skirt panels into even pleats, baste. Attach skirt to sofa cover. Hem lower edge and ends of skirt (*see diagram 2*). If desired, sew a button to top of each pleat.

Tied-under Finish

If no skirt is required, a tied-under finish will hold the lower edge of the sofa cover in place.

Measure and make cover sections for outside back, outside arms, front arms and front to fit to bottom edge of sofa.

Cut pieces to fit along each bottom section by about 8 inches wide, for tie-under flaps. Stitch flaps to lower edge of each section, trim excess fabric so that flaps clear the sofa feet. Zigzag raw edges. Stitch a 5/8-inch wide casing along long edges of flaps. Thread a length of cotton tape through casings on flaps. Fit cover to sofa, fold flaps under seat and tie in position with tape (*see diagram 3*).

DIAGRAM 3

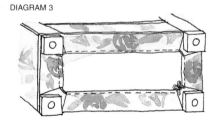

SKIRT FINISHES

Gathered Skirt Finish

Cut skirt pieces depth required plus 5/8-inch seam allowance and 2 inches for double hem (see instructions on page 127), and twice the finished width. Stitch two rows of gathering along one long edge. Pull up gathers to fit sofa cover edge. Pin skirt edge along bottom edge of sofa cover, right sides together, concentrating extra gathers at corners. Stitch skirt to sofa cover, zigzag edge. Stitch hem along lower edge of skirt (*see diagram 1*).

Pleated Skirt Finish

Calculate depth of skirt panels, adding 5/8-inch seam allowance to top and 2 inches for double hem. To total width of each panel, add 8 inches for each pleat plus 2 inches for each

DIAGRAM 1

DIAGRAM 2

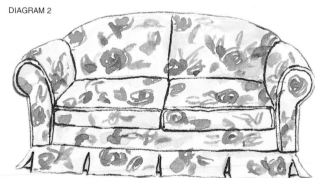

RE-COVERING A CHAIR WITH UPHOLSTERED SEAT

- 🌑 upholstery fabric
- 🌑 calico (for under seat)
- 🌑 batting
- 🌑 strong thread
- 🌑 tailor's chalk
- 🌑 upholstery needle
- 🌑 upholstery tacks
- 🌑 small tacks
- 🌑 braid (optional)

Measure the seat and sides and add 3 inches on all edges, for seat piece. Measure underneath seat and add ¾ inch on all edges, for lining under seat. Cut one seat piece from upholstery fabric and one lining piece from calico.

Remove old cover from seat. If there is a thin layer of batting, remove this too. Trim new batting to fit seat, place on seat and secure with large basting stitches. Mark the center of fabric and chair with chalk and place the new cover fabric on seat, matching centers.

Fix fabric to seat frame with a few evenly spaced upholstery tacks at each side of the chair (see diagram 1).

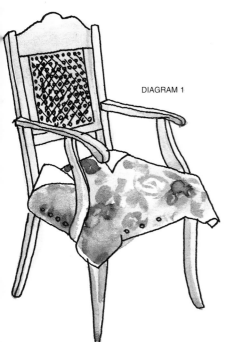

DIAGRAM 1

Fold over corner of fabric next to the back uprights to right side. Clip fabric from the corner to the fold (see diagram 2).

DIAGRAM 2

Fold fabric around upright, trim excess fabric from corners, leaving ¾ inch allowance for hem fold. Fold allowance under and tack fabric to frame next to chair legs. Clip fabric to fit around uprights in similar fashion.

Fold excess fabric at each of the front corners into a pleat, making sure foldline falls at the corner edge of chair (see diagram 3). Adjust tacks if necessary to give a smooth, even finish, adding extra tacks if required.

DIAGRAM 3

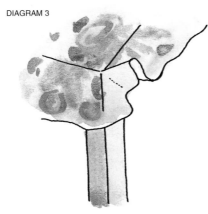

Pull fabric around bottom edge of seat frame, tack in place under the frame using small tacks, trim excess. Press under ¾ inch allowance all around calico. Tack calico in place

under seat, over raw edges of cover fabric. Clip and trim fabric around legs as for uprights.

If seat is deep, slip-stitch the fold of the front corner pleat in place using upholstery needle and strong thread.

Optional finish

If the chair has a decorative frame, fabric can be tacked to the top edge of the frame and trimmed below the tacks. Braid can be glued over to give neat finish. Fold under ⅜ inch on one end of braid and place a tack inside the fold. Tack braid end over fabric edge (see diagram 4), glue braid in place around the frame securing with another tack, as before, at other end.

DIAGRAM 4

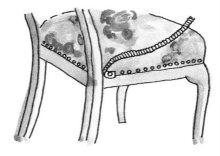

SLIP COVER FOR WINGED CHAIR

- 🍃 7²/₃ *yards furnishing fabric (less will be required if you do not wish to add piping)*
- 🍃 *approximately 16¹/₂ yards heavy jute twine, for piping*
- 🍃 *strong pins*
- 🍃 *19-inch zipper*
- 🍃 *1¹/₂ yards cotton tape, for leg ties*

Note: When you are cutting and fitting, do not follow the original upholstery stitchlines of the chair, as they will not correspond with the stitchlines of a slip cover.

It is important that the pattern of the fabric runs in the right direction for all your pieces. Avoid using checked or striped fabrics that will be difficult to match.

Buy pre-shrunk fabric for washing purposes. If you are using a fabric that is likely to shrink when washed, allow an inch or two at every seam to counteract shrinkage, or shrink fabric in water before starting to cut and sew.

The instructions refer to the parts of the chair shown in *diagram 1*.

General instructions

If you are a beginner or if your chair is an unusual shape, fit and cut the pieces for the chair from calico or old sheeting before attempting to make the cover from selected fabric. Cut all the length measurements on the lengthwise grain of the fabric and all the width measurements on the cross grain. As you cut each piece mark with a pencil, on the wrong side, the direction of the grain and the name of the section.

As you fit each piece overestimate the amount of fabric needed by an inch or two, pin piece in place on chair, then trim fabric to the correct seam allowance.

Measuring, cutting and pinning

To make cutting easier, take only half-width measurements when measuring chair. Most pieces can then be cut on the fold, or the measurements can simply be doubled.

First find the vertical center line of the chair *(see photo 1)*. Start by measuring across the front border and place a pin at the half-width mark. Continue placing pins at the half-width mark across the seat, then up the inside back, over the top of the back and down the outside back. At this stage there is no need to take measurements for the arm pieces or the sides of the chair.

Measure the height of the inside back. Allow 1 inch at the top for a seam, 6 inches at the bottom for the tuck, and 1¹/₂ inches on the side edges for tucks *(see diagram 2)*.

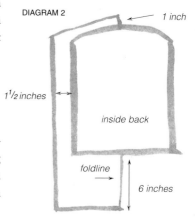

DIAGRAM 2

1 inch

1¹/₂ inches

inside back

foldline

6 inches

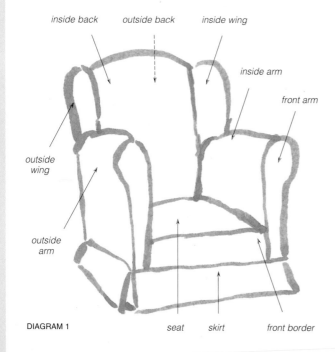

inside back   outside back   inside wing

inside arm

front arm

outside wing

outside arm

DIAGRAM 1   seat   skirt   front border

1

If your winged chair does not have space for a tuck in between the inside back and the inside wing, you do not have to allow for the tuck – keep side seams to 1 inch. Cut out fabric to correct size on the fold, with right sides together.

Pin cut piece in position on chair, using center marking pins as a guide *(see photo 2)*. Leave piece on chair.

Mark the center line of the back of the chair with pins and measure the height of the outside back *(see photo 3)*. Cut out fabric to correct size on the fold with right sides together. Allow 1 inch for seams on all sides.

Measure the width of the seat, add 6 inches at back edge for tuck, 1½

inches at the front of the side edges – widening to 6 inches for tuck at the back – and 1 inch at front edge for seam allowance *(see diagram 3)*. Fit to seat of chair with pins *(see photo 4)*.

Fit the front border piece and pin. Pin seams together as you go and trim the fabric back to a 1 inch seam allowance. When cutting the arm and

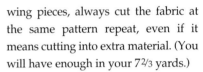

DIAGRAM 3

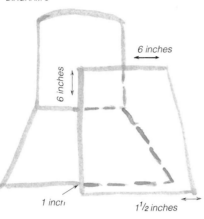

6 inches

6 inches

1 inch

1½ inches

wing pieces, always cut the fabric at the same pattern repeat, even if it means cutting into extra material. (You will have enough in your 7⅔ yards.)

Measure the outside arm section from the base of the chair up to the

outside curve of the arm top *(see photo 5)*. Cut four lengths across the full width of the fabric by the height of the outside arm. These lengths will be used for making two outside arm pieces, two inside arm pieces, and the two outside and two inside wings of the chair.

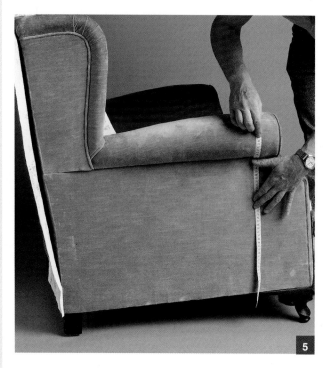

Pin outside arm pieces in position. Trim off excess fabric that is hanging at the back *(see photo 6)* – this will be used for the outside wings. Pin inside arm pieces in position. Note 6-inch seam allowance at the back that tapers along the side seam to 1½ inches at front of seam. Excess fabric from this piece will be used to make pieces for inside wings.

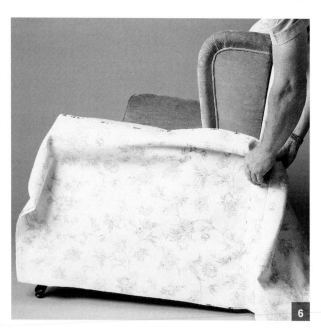

Start fitting the outside wing, using excess fabric from the outside arm. Pin fabric in place, leaving any extra fabric hanging at the back *(see photo 7a)*. The outside wing piece should be pinned to the outside back, to the outside arm and around the front shaping of the wing. Trim seams to 1 inch *(see photo 7b)*. Excess fabric will be used for the inside wing, and any left after that may be enough to fit the front arm section.

When fitting around the top section of the inside wings, make several evenly spaced darts to allow for the shaping *(see photo 8a)*. Note that seam allowances on the inside edges of the inside wings will have to be tapered to allow for tucks *(see photo 8b)*. Use the shaping you have already cut for the inside back as your guide, before cutting the inside wing pieces. Pin these pieces in place and trim seams appropriately.

If you have a chair that does not leave room for a tuck, do not allow for one now. Run piping along the seam when it comes to stitching.

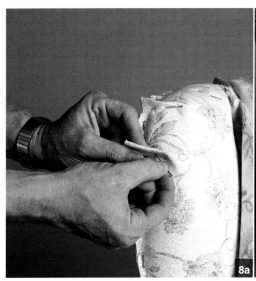

If you still have fabric left over after fitting the wings, check to see if there is enough to fit the arm fronts. This will depend on the width of fabric, the pattern repeat and the size of chair. If you have insufficient fabric, measure the front arm, adding 1 or 2 inches for leeway, and cut it from your roll, making sure that the grain and pattern of the fabric run in the same direction as the front border.

Pin front arms in place and trim seams *(see photo 9)*, leaving a 1-inch seam allowance on all sides.

Note: At this stage, it is a good idea to notch or cut out little triangles along all seamlines so that you can match the seams accurately when you are stitching. You will have noticed that quite a bit of easing has been required to fit the pieces together well. Notching the seams will ensure the correct shape is maintained as you stitch.

Chances are the lower edge of the chair is not straight, so do not use it as your guide to trimming the lower edge of the cover. Measure along the lower edge of the chair as though you were taking up the hem of a dress, measuring from the ground up *(see photo 10a)*. Using a pencil, mark the same measurement around all four sides. Trim along this line *(see photo 10b)*.

Unpinning

Before removing all the fabric pieces for stitching, use a pencil to label all the pieces on the wrong side – inside back, outside back and so on. Mark around all the darts so that you can see where they should go after you have removed the pins. You might also like to color code, or note on the pieces, which seams join which.

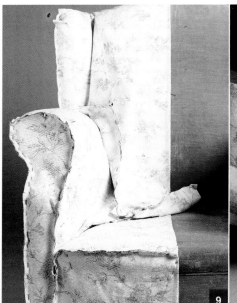

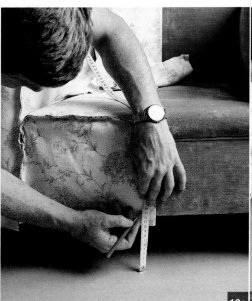

DIAGRAM 4

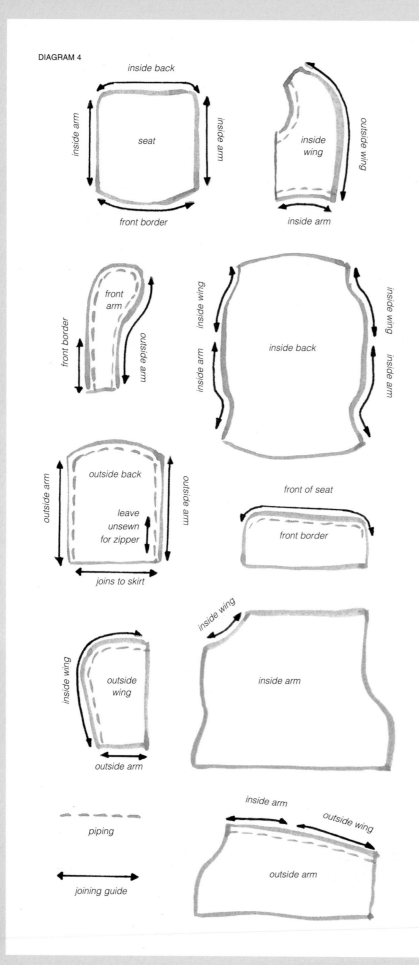

Measuring skirt and preparing piping

Check that you have all the pieces required to make the slip cover – that you have two front arms, two inside arms, two outside arms and so on. Measure the cushion and allow as much fabric as will be required, not forgetting to include generous seam allowances.

Before cutting piping, work out how much fabric you need for the skirt. Measure each side of the slip cover, add these measurements together, then add 32 inches, plus seam allowance, to your final measurement to allow for 8 inches of inverted pleat at each corner. If you have to join your fabric to get the correct width, you will have to allow for more than one seam allowance. Make sure the joining seams fall within the inverted pleats. The depth of the skirt will depend on how much you wish to allow for the hem, and how much drop is required to meet the floor. Add 1 inch for your top seam allowance and make allowance for the hem.

Cut out the amount of fabric required and set aside. The rest of your fabric can now be used for piping. Cut and join bias strips 1½ inches wide, and use jute to make approximately 15½ yards of corded piping (see instructions on page 125). *Diagram 4* shows to which seams the piping can be stitched. Following instructions on page 125, apply the piping to the front arms, outside wings, outside arms and the outside back pieces.

Stitch darts on inside wing pieces.

Stitching

When stitching pieces together, refer to *diagram 5* for sequence.

Lay out your pieces in front of you so that you can clearly see the label on each piece. When you are stitching seams that have been piped, keep

DIAGRAM 5

right sides together, sandwiching the piping in between. Turn the material over so that you can see the stitching line of the piping, and stitch seam along this line.

First, join the inside wing to the inside arm (a). Join the inside back to inside arms and inside wings (b). Stitch the seat in place, starting at the front of the inside arm seam, stitching across the back, joining the inside back, then stitching down the inside arm seam on the opposite side (c).

Join the front border piece to the front section of the seat (d). Join the outside wing to the inside wing (e). Join the outside arm to the inside arm; run stitching on to the outside wing (f). Join front arms, starting at front border, stitching up inside arm and down outside arm (g). Join outside back. Stitch the back corner seam, over the top of the chair and down the other back corner seam, leaving one corner seam open for at least 19 inches to accommodate zipper (h). Insert zipper.

Stitch piping around all base edges. Take up the hem of the fabric you have cut for the skirt. Pin inverted pleats in place so that there is an inverted pleat over each corner of the chair *(see diagram 6)*. Check against the chair before stitching. Stitch skirt onto lower edge of cover.

Cut tape into 12-inch lengths. Slip-stitch at seam under each inverted pleat to make ties for legs. Ties will prevent seat cover from slipping.

DIAGRAM 6

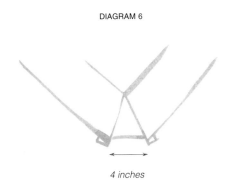

4 inches

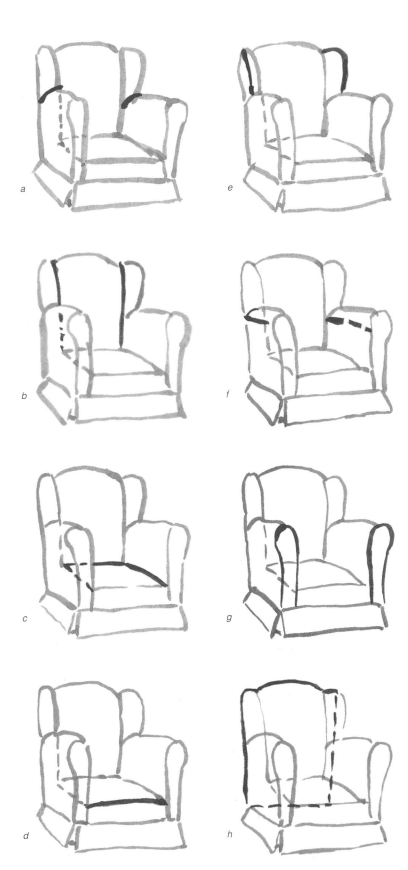

BACK PLEATED SLIP COVER

❦ *2 1/4 yards x 54"-wide striped drill* ❦ *thread*

Note: Measure each section of the chair at its longest and widest points – **diagram 1** shows where the measurements for each piece are taken – then use these measurements to make paper patterns.

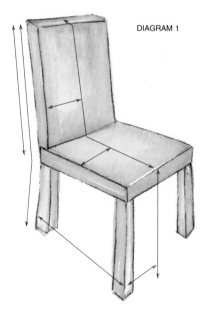

DIAGRAM 1

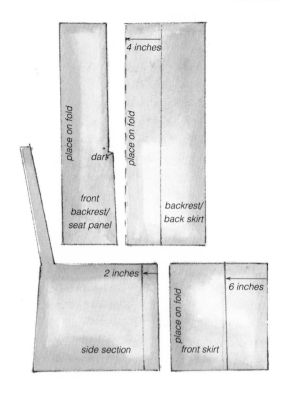

DIAGRAM 2

4 inches

place on fold

place on fold

dart

front backrest/ seat panel

backrest/ back skirt

2 inches

side section

place on fold

6 inches

front skirt

Measuring, pattern making and cutting

Refer to **diagram 2** for an indication of what the finished patterns look like.

Measure the half-width and the full depth of seat, then measure the half-width and full height of the inside backrest. Use measurements to cut half pattern for the front backrest/ seat panel, adding a dart in the backrest/seat panel junction as shown in **diagram 2**.

Measure height of outside back from top of chair to floor, following the curve of the chair. Measure the half-width of outside back, then cut a half pattern for backrest/back skirt, adding 4 inches to center back for center inverted pleat.

Measure the half-width of the chair at the widest point of the front and the height from the seat to the floor, then cut a half pattern for the front skirt, adding on 6 inches for the inverted pleat at either side.

Measure the width of the chair at the side, and the height from the seat to the floor, then cut a pattern for the side skirt, adding 2 inches to front of skirt for front corner pleats. Measure the width of the uprights and their height from the chair seat to the top of the uprights, then cut from paper. Attach uprights piece to side skirt at an angle that suits back curve of chair – pin pattern to chair to achieve correct curve of side section.

Fold the fabric in half lengthwise. When placing pattern pieces on the fabric, make sure that the stripes of corresponding pattern pieces continue unbroken when stitched together.

Place the center line of the front backrest/seat panel and front skirt on fold. Place the foldline of the pleat of backrest/back skirt on fold. The side section is the only piece that is not cut on the fold.

Add 5/8-inch seam allowances around all pattern pieces and 2 inches to hems. Cut from fabric.

Stitching

Press inverted pleat of backrest/back skirt in position. With right sides together, stitch along front foldlines for about 8 inches (*see diagram 3*). Return pleat to finished position and baste along upper seamline.

DIAGRAM 3

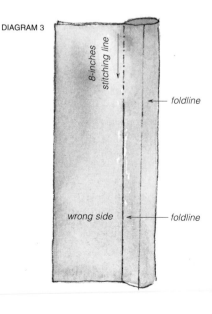

8-inches stitching line

foldline

wrong side

foldline

With right sides together, stitch front skirt to side panels. Fold and press side pleats of skirt in position (*see diagram 4*). Stitch, on right side, along the foldlines, about 8 inches.

Stitch darts of seat panel in position. With right sides together, stitch front skirt to front backrest/seat panel. Stitch side panels to front backrest/seat panel. Cut into seam allowance of front backrest at corners. Press seam allowance towards seat and front backrest, topstitch seams.

Stitch the backrest/back skirt panel to corresponding side of side panels and along top edge of front backrest,

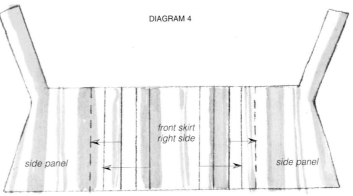

DIAGRAM 4

front skirt
right side

side panel

side panel

right sides together. Press seam allowance towards backrest/back skirt panel, topstitch seam.

Turn cover through to the right side. Finish bottom edge of skirt with a 2-inch hem. Slip cover over chair.

DIRECTOR'S CHAIR COVERS

One-piece Director's Chair Cover

- *1 yard x 36"-wide fabric (we used canvas)*
- *thread*
- *upholstery tacks or staple gun*

Note: Our fabric piece measured 34" x 28" (including seam allowance). Chair sizes may vary, so check these measurements to make sure they are right for your frame.

Measure chair and mark out the basic rectangular shape on fabric. To calculate the width of the fabric piece, measure around one chair back post, across the open frame and around the other chair back post.

To calculate the length of the fabric piece, measure from 1 1/2 inches below the upright, down the inside back of the chair, and from the back to the front of the seat.

On each side of the rectangular piece, 8 inches below the top edge, mark a curved section 5 inches wide and 11 inches long *(see diagram)*. Add 3/8-inch seam allowance to all edges before cutting.

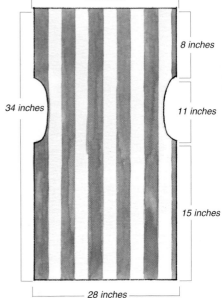

Zigzag raw edges and stitch a 3/8-inch hem along all edges of the fabric piece, including the cut-out curved section at the sides.

Turn under and pin a 2 1/2-inch casing along the side edge above the cut-out curved section. Fit the cover onto the chair back posts, check the fit, and adjust casing if necessary. Remove the cover and double-stitch the casing in place.

Replace the cover on the chair, pull the side edges of the seat around to the underside of the seat frame, hold in place with a couple of tacks or staples. Fold the frame closed and fix the seat in place underneath the seat frame with tacks or staples.

Fix the back of the cover at desired height, then tack or staple it to the chair back posts.

Two-piece Director's Chair Cover

- 🐦 *²/3 yard x 36"-wide fabric (we used canvas)*
- 🐦 *thread*
- 🐦 *upholstery tacks or staple gun*

Note: Our back piece measured 28" x 8", and the seat piece measured 23" x 16" (including seam allowance). Chair sizes may vary, so check these measurements to make sure they are right for your chair.

Remove the old cover, take out the seams and use it as a pattern for the new cover.

If there is no old cover, calculate width of back piece by measuring around one chair back post, across open front and around second chair back post. Calculate depth of back piece as required. Add ³/8-inch seam allowance around all sides, and cut back piece from fabric.

Measure the seat frame, adding allowance to width for tacking fabric to the underside of the frame at each side, plus ³/8-inch hem allowance to all edges. Cut seat piece from fabric.

Zigzag raw edges and stitch a ³/8-inch hem along all sides of the back piece. Turn under and pin a 2 ½-inch casing on each short side. Place back piece onto the chair posts, check fit

and adjust the casing if necessary. Remove back piece, and double-stitch casing in place *(see diagram 1)*.

Replace the back on the chair, and fix it at the desired height by either tacking or stapling it to the back of the chair posts.

Zigzag raw edges and stitch a ³/8-inch hem along all sides of seat piece. Place the seat piece on the chair, pull the side edges around to the underside of the seat frame, hold in place with a couple of tacks or staples. Fold frame closed and fix seat in place with tacks or staples *(see diagram 2)*.

DIAGRAM 1

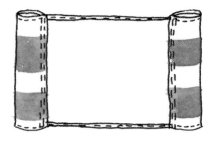

DIAGRAM 2

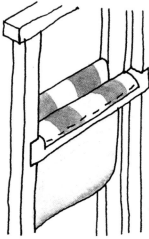

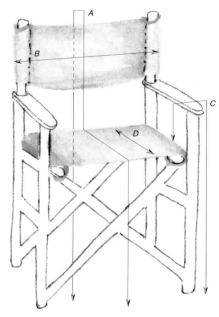

Tie-on Cover for Director's Chair

❧ *2 1/2 yards x 45"-wide fabric*
❧ *thread*

Note: Our main fabric piece measured 87" x 23", and side pieces measured 35" x 20" (including seam allowance). Chair sizes vary, so check these measurements to make sure they are right for your chair.

To calculate the length of main fabric piece, measure from the floor at back of chair to top of chair back posts, down inside back, from back of seat to front and down to the floor *(see A on diagram)*. To calculate the width of main fabric piece, measure across back of chair from outside edge of one chair back post to outside edge of the other *(see B on diagram)*.

To calculate the length of side pieces, measure from side edge of seat, up over arm and down to the floor *(see C on diagram)*. To calculate the width of side pieces, measure from back of seat to front of seat *(see D on diagram)*.

Add ³/₈-inch seam allowance around all edges. Cut one main piece and two side pieces. Cut four 28" x 3" pieces, for ties.

Place main fabric piece in position on chair, wrong side up. Place a pin at top of chair posts, seat back and seat front to mark these positions. Pin fabric edges together from top of chair posts to arms, pinning a ³/₈-inch seam allowance. Remove and stitch pinned seams.

Replace main piece on chair; pins should be in correct positions. Pin narrow edge of each side piece to main piece, between back of seat and front of seat markings. Fold fabric over arm, pin side edges together from top of arm to point where side piece joins main piece at seat edge. From this point to floor, pin side piece to main piece; edges at floor level should be even. Remove cover, stitch pinned seams.

At top of each arm, pin a small seam across the folded edge at the front, at right angles to the seam running down the front. Stitch and trim. Zigzag all raw edges on seams. Zigzag remaining raw edges, turn under and stitch a ³/₈-inch hem.

Zigzag raw edges then stitch a ³/₈-inch hem on the long edges and one narrow edge of tie pieces. Pin a tie to each side of main piece level with back of arms. Pin a tie to side piece at back to correspond. Stitch in place. Turn cover right side out, place over chair and tie bows at the back.

QUICK CHAIR COVER

- 2 3/4 *yards x 45"-wide fabric*
- 3 1/4 *yards ribbon, for bows*
- *pins*
- *thread*

Note: If using patterned fabric, be sure to center the design of the fabric on each rectangle.

Calculate the size of the first rectangle. Measure from the floor at the front of the chair, up to and across the seat, then up and over the backrest and down to the floor at the back of the chair *(see photo 1)*. Add 2-inch hem allowance to this length. Measure the width of the chair, adding 1 1/2 inches to cover chair frame and 2 inches for side hems. Cut rectangle from fabric.

Now find the size of the second rectangle. Measure from the floor on one side of the chair to the floor on the other side, taking the tape up to and across the seat. Add 2-inch hem allowance to this length. Calculate width of rectangle by measuring from the back to the front of the seat and adding on 2-inch side hem allowance. Cut rectangle from fabric.

Zigzag raw edges, then turn up and stitch 1-inch hems on all sides of both rectangles. Press.

Drape rectangles over chair, the first over the chair's length *(see photo 2)*, the second over the seat *(see photo 3)*.

Cut twelve 10-inch lengths of ribbon. Pin one ribbon to back of first rectangle where seat joins back of the chair and one on seat edge of second rectangle. Pin a pair of ribbons on the other side, a pair on each of the two front corners of the seat, and the remaining pair between the seat and the top of the chair. Tie ribbons into six bows, securing the two rectangles.

SCALLOPED-EDGE TABLE SETTING

Tablecloth with Scalloped Edge

🐦 1¹/₂ yards x 54"-wide fabric (we used damask)
🐦 thread
🐦 water-erasable marking pen
🐦 cardboard
🐦 typing paper

Finished size: 53"-square; tablecloth fits 36"-square table.

Make scalloped cardboard template by drawing semi-circles along the edge of the cardboard using a glass as a guide. Trim cardboard edge into scalloped pattern.

   Trace scallops along all edges of the fabric with a water-erasable marking pen, positioning tops of scallops ³/₈ inch from edge of fabric.

   Using closely spaced zigzag (satin) stitch, stitch along marked line, turning fabric between each scallop. Trim fabric close to stitching *(see diagram)*. Clip between scallops and stitch again, if necessary.

Note: If fabric puckers when stitching, place a strip of typing paper underneath fabric. Remove paper when stitching is complete.

Napkin with Scalloped Edge

Cut a 16-inch square of fabric (we used damask) and make as for Tablecloth with Scalloped Edge.

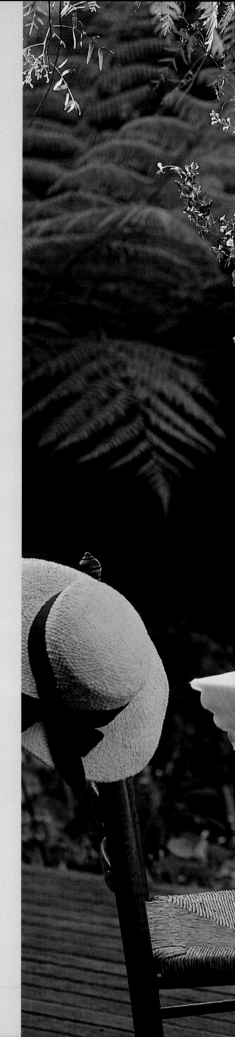

TABLE LINEN

Dress up a table with a ruffled, flounced or scalloped-edged
cloth – it is easily made, yet instantly brightens any setting.
Also included are instructions for making pretty placemats and
embroidered napkins, plus simple decorating tips: overlay
several lace-edged cloths, stitch on a tasseled fringe, or add a
border of grosgrain ribbon or a contrasting binding to transform
a simple tablecloth into a splendid table accessory.

MEASURING FOR TABLECLOTHS

If the diameter or width of your cloth is greater than the fabric width, you will have to join your fabric. This is usually done by joining a strip along each side of the center piece, avoiding seams in the cloth center.

Square

Measure across table (a) and add twice the overhang measurement (b). Overhang can be to your lap or to the floor. Include hem allowance in overhang measurement.

Rectangular

Measure across table (a) and add twice the overhang measurement (b) to calculate width. Measure across table (c) and add twice overhang (b) to calculate length. Include hem allowance in overhang measurement.

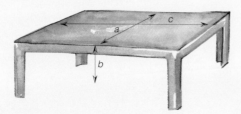

Round

Measure diameter of table (a) and add twice the overhang measurement (b). Overhang can be to your lap, to the floor, or longer to drape over the floor. Include hem allowance in overhang measurement.

TABLE ROUND WITH OVERLAY

DIAGRAM 2

For tablecloth

- *4¹/₂ yards x 45"-wide fabric*
  (we used chintz)
- *thread*
- *string*
- *pencil*

Finished size: Approximately 80"-diameter; tablecloth fits 30"-high, 20"-diameter table.

Cut fabric into two 2¹/₄-yard lengths. Cut one length in half lengthwise to give two 22¹/₂-inch-wide lengths. ³/₈ inch seam allowance is included.

With right sides together, stitch the 22¹/₂-inch-wide lengths to each side of large fabric piece *(see diagram 1)*. Edge-finish raw edges; press.

DIAGRAM 1

Fold fabric in half lengthwise and then in half crosswise. Tie one end of a piece of string to a pencil and pin the other end to center of fabric piece. Adjust string to measure 40 inches. Mark a quarter circle with a 40-inch radius on fabric *(see diagram 2)*.

Cut along pencil line through all layers of fabric.

Zigzag raw edge and stitch a ³/₈-inch hem around tablecloth edge; press.

For overlay

- *1¹/₄ yards x 45"-wide fabric*
- *thread*

Finished size: Approximately 40"-square.

Cut 41"-square of fabric. ³/₈-inch seam allowance is included. Zigzag raw edges. Turn under and stitch a narrow hem around all edges of fabric; press.

STRIPED TABLE SET

Striped Placemats

For four placemats:

🐦 *1 yard x 45"-wide solid-colored fabric*
🐦 *¼ yard x 60"-wide striped fabric*
🐦 *¾ yard x 36"-wide fusible interfacing*
🐦 *thread*

Finished size: 16" x 12".

For each placemat, cut a 21" x 17" solid-colored fabric piece, 12½" x 8½" striped fabric piece and 16" x 12" interfacing piece. ⅜-inch seam allowance is included.

Fuse interfacing to center of wrong side of plain fabric, leaving a border of fabric. Fold in and press border towards interfaced side of placemat *(see diagram 1)*.

DIAGRAM 1

Turn under seam allowance along raw edge of border, press. Fold under corners of fabric allowance to give a "mitered" or "dovetailed" border *(see diagram 2)*.

DIAGRAM 2

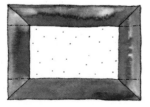

Center striped fabric piece over interfacing and under border edge. Pin then baste to hold in position. Stitch close to folded edges at corners and around inside border, through all layers of fabric *(see diagram 3)*.

DIAGRAM 3

Rectangular Tablecloth with Ruffle

🐦 *1¾ yards x 45"-wide solid-colored fabric*
🐦 *2 yards x 60"-widestriped fabric*
🐦 *thread*

Finished size: 82" x 58"; cloth fits 60" x 36" table.

Note: Calculate your fabric requirements and cut pieces according to your table size.

Cut one 61" x 37" solid-colored fabric piece for top of cloth, or same size as table top, adding ⅜-inch seam allowance to all sides. Cut six 60" x 12" striped fabric strips for ruffle, or cut enough 12-inch-wide strips, including seam allowances, to make, when joined, a ruffle about twice the outer measurement of tablecloth top.

With right sides together, join narrow ends of ruffle strips to make a continuous loop. Zigzag raw edges and stitch a narrow hem along one long edge of ruffle strip.

Stitch two rows of gathering along raw edge. Pull up gathers to fit plain fabric piece. Pin ruffle around plain fabric piece, right sides facing, easing gathers evenly. Stitch, edge-finish raw edges and press.

Napkin with Ruffle

🐦 *12"-square solid-colored fabric*
🐦 *¼ yard x 60"-wide striped fabric*
🐦 *thread*

Finished size: 16-inch square, approximately.

Cut and join 3-inch-wide striped fabric strips to give a 90-inch-long ruffle strip. ⅜-inch seam allowance is included.

With right sides together, join narrow ends of ruffle strip. Stitch a narrow hem along one long edge of ruffle strip.

Stitch two rows of gathering along raw edge. Pull up gathers to fit around plain fabric piece. Pin ruffle to plain fabric piece, right sides facing, concentrating gathers at corners. Stitch, edge-finish raw edges and press.

TABLE ROUND
WITH RUFFLE

- 🌿 *4 yards x 54"-wide fabric*
  - 🍂 *thread*
  - 🌿 *string*
  - 🍂 *pencil*

Finished size: 75-inch-diameter, approximately; cloth fits 28-inch-high, 18-inch-diameter table. For a full-length table round, cut your cloth with an approximate diameter four times that of the table.

Cut one 70" x 54" fabric piece and two 70" x 8" fabric pieces for cloth. Cut and join 5-inch-wide fabric strips to create a ruffle strip approximately twice the circumference of the cloth. ³⁄₈-inch seam allowance is included.

With right sides together, stitch the 8-inch-wide pieces to each side of the 54-inch-wide piece along the 70-inch edges (*see diagram 1*, Table Round with Overlay on page 65). Edge-finish seam allowances and press.

Following instructions for Table Round with Overlay, fold fabric in half lengthwise and then crosswise. Using a string and pencil, draw a

quarter circle with a 34-inch radius (*see diagram 2*, Table Round with Overlay). Cut out cloth.

With right sides facing, stitch the ends of the ruffle strip to form a continuous loop. Stitch a narrow hem on one edge of the ruffle.

Stitch two rows of gathering along raw edge of ruffle, and pull up into gathers. Fold the ruffle and the cloth into quarters and mark these points with pins.

With right sides together, pin ruffle to cloth, matching pins and easing gathers evenly. Stitch ruffle to cloth. Edge-finish raw edges, press.

▼ *Color and texture are juxtaposed in a spirited interpretation of the standard flowery tablecloth. The shape of the cloth is strongly defined by a dark green grosgrain border, while the edge is embellished with tassels. In place of a corded fabric such as grosgrain, a matte or shiny trim could be used to create a different effect.*

▲ *The strong pattern on this floor-length tablecloth is crisply accented by a plain, bound edging. This could echo one of the colors in the cloth or be chosen as a contrast.*

▼ *Mixing and matching patterns can produce stunning effects. The stronger the colors used, the bolder the look, as this circular, floor-length cloth topped with a short overlay demonstrates. The scalloped edge detail adds extra interest.*

▲ *Romantic lace makes a great combination with full-blown florals, creating a charming setting for china and flowers reminiscent of the Victorian and Edwardian eras. The full-length round undercloth is covered with a square white cloth trimmed with handkerchief-points of lace, then topped by another white square featuring a scalloped lace edging.*

TABLECLOTHS

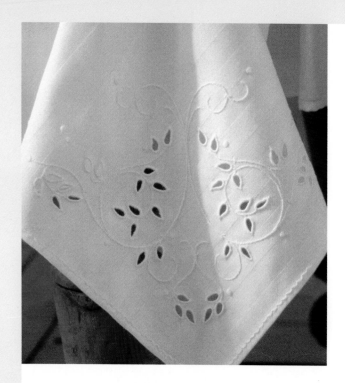

Work satin stitch around the leaf shapes, working over the running stitch outline and folding the cut fabric behind and into the stitches as you work *(see diagram 2)*. Keep satin stitching close and even.

Using two strands of embroidery floss, work tendrils and stems in stem stitch (see page 126), and small dots in satin stitch.

Finish the edge of the cloth with a decorative row of stitching, by threading three strands of embroidery floss in and out of every other stitch of the machine stitching around the hem.

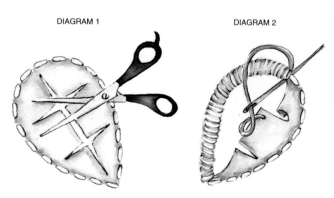

DIAGRAM 1   DIAGRAM 2

Napkins

Work cutwork design on napkins in same manner as the tablecloth, but use only the section of the design to the right of dotted line and work only one corner of each napkin. Position design approximately 1 inch from napkin edges. Use your own judgment when adding small dots to the design. Work decorative border in same manner as the tablecloth.

CUTWORK TABLE LINEN

❧ *white ready-made tablecloth and napkins*
*(see **Note**, below)*
❧ *DMC Pearl Cotton No. 8: white*
❧ *white six-strand cotton embroidery floss*
❧ *tracing paper*
❧ *tailor's carbon paper*
❧ *fine, sharp scissors*

Note: Purchase a tablecloth and napkins, or make your own from white cotton damask or linen. We used a self-striped cotton damask.

Finished size: Our tablecloth is approximately 70" x 77", napkins are 16 inches square.

Tablecloth

Enlarge the design on a photocopier following instructions on diagram, then trace the full-size design onto tracing paper. Using tailor's carbon paper, transfer the outline to each corner of the tablecloth, positioning it approximately 1½ inches from the edges.

Using Pearl Cotton, work around the outline of each tiny leaf in evenly spaced running stitch. Work second row of running stitch over first row, filling in spaces and entering and exiting by same holes. Clip into the center of each leaf using fine, sharp scissors, taking care to cut almost as far as, but not into, the stitching itself *(see diagram 1)*.

Enlarge on photocopier at 200%, then enlarge the result at 150%.

PLACEMATS

Quilted Placemats

For each placemat:

🌢 *18" x 12" fabric*

🌢 *18" x 12" contrasting fabric*

🌢 *18" x 12" medium-weight batting*

🌢 *approximately 1³/4 yards x 1"-wide bias binding, or make your own following instructions on page 125*

🌢 *thread*

Cut pattern using a piece of paper measuring 18" x 12" folded into quarters *(see diagram 1)*. Pin one end of a piece of string at a point 6 inches in from A, and tie a pencil to other end of string. Draw an arc to make an oval.

Cut one piece of main fabric, one piece of contrasting fabric and one piece of batting.

Sandwich the batting between the main fabric piece and contrasting fabric piece, right sides facing outwards. Starting at the center and working towards the edge, baste the three layers together. Using a large stitch, machine quilt the layers together – you can either stitch around a design on the fabric or create a freeform design as you go.

Fold over ³/8 inch to the wrong side on one end of the bias binding *(see diagram 2)*. Apply binding to napkin edge following instructions on page 125. You will need to clip binding carefully to ease around corners.

DIAGRAM 2

DIAGRAM 1

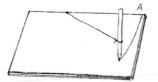

Placemats with Corded Trim

For each placemat:

☙ *20" x 14" double-sided fabric*

☙ *crochet cotton*

☙ *thread*

Press under 1 inch all around placemat. Miter or dovetail corners following instructions on page 125, then stitch hem in place, close to inner raw edge. Trim fabric close to stitching.

With dovetailed corners facing upwards, lay a strand of crochet cotton along the stitching line and, using wide, closely spaced zigzag setting, stitch over cotton *(see diagram)*, concealing raw edges at the same time. Square off at the corners and, before completing the last inch of stitching, cut the crochet cotton so that the ends join neatly.

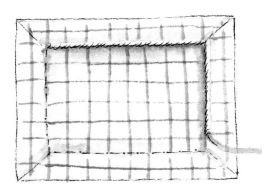

NAPKINS

Lace-edged Napkin

Overcast the edges of a square of fabric with narrow zigzag stitch. Pin 1-inch-wide cotton lace edging around the edge of the square, right sides together, leaving a "loop" twice the width of the lace at each corner and a 1-inch overhang at beginning and end. Stitch into place with a narrow zigzag stitch. Open out lace and stitch a diagonal line between inner and outer edges at each corner. Edge-finish mitered seams, press napkin seam allowances towards fabric, then top-stitch around napkin close to seam.

Fringed Napkin

Cut napkin square on a pulled edge to straighten edges. Stitch 1 inch in from raw edges with narrow, closely spaced zigzag. Carefully pull out threads up to the stitching line.

Hem-stitched Napkin

Cut napkin square on a pulled edge to straighten edges. Measure in 2 inches around all edges of napkin, tack to mark outer edge of border, then measure in ¼ inch and baste to mark inner edge of border. Using sharp embroidery scissors, cut the horizontal fabric threads at each end of each marked border. Draw out required number of threads with tapestry needle (*see diagram 1*). The corners will be secured by buttonhole stitch.

Press under ¼ inch on raw edges of napkin. Press hem so that fold is just below first row of drawn threads. Miter or dovetail corners following instructions on page 125.

Following instructions for hem stitch on page 126 and working from left to right, hem stitch outer edges of border first, catching hem in stitches. To secure, pass thread through completed stitches. Hem stitch inner edges, finishing the same way.

Knot bundles together as desired, hiding the thread. (We knotted ours in groups of two – *see diagram 2*).

DIAGRAM 1

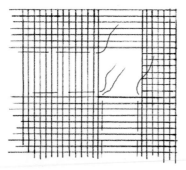

DIAGRAM 2

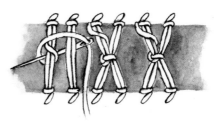

Finish corners by working buttonhole stitch (see page 126) to reinforce corner edges.

Bound Napkin

Round the edges of a fabric square. A saucer makes a good template. Make and apply contrasting bias binding in fabric following instructions on page 125.

Double-stitched Napkin

Turn under ¼ inch around edge of napkin, press. Turn under 1-inch hem, pin or baste. Using wing needle, stitch from corner of stitching line to edge of napkin. With tip of needle in fabric, pivot, return over previous stitching, continue to next stitching-line corner, then stitch to edge of napkin. Pivot, return to stitching line, pivot, stitch to other edge, pivot, then continue to next corner (*see diagram 3*). Repeat until napkin is hemmed.

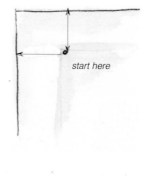

start here

Napkin with Corded Trim

Trim raw edges, then press under 1 inch all around napkin. Miter corners following instructions on page 125 and stitch hem in place, close to raw edge. Trim fabric close to stitching.

With mitered corners facing upwards, lay a strand of crochet cotton along the stitching line and, using wide, closely spaced zigzag setting, stitch over cotton (*see diagram*, Placemat with Corded Trim, on page 73). Square off at the corners and, before completing the last inch of stitching, cut the crochet cotton so that the ends join neatly.

BONDED LAMPSHADES

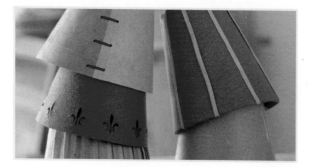

Cutting a pattern

To make a pattern, you will need pattern paper, pencil and ruler. Place frame on pattern paper and mark the position of one strut and top and bottom ring. Also make a pencil mark on the first strut. Carefully roll the frame, drawing positions of top and bottom rings, until you have a complete outline of frame *(see diagram)*. Add seam allowances according to instructions for individual lampshades.

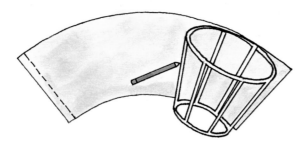

Lampshade with Braid Trim

🦀 *thin cardboard* 🦀 *fabric*
🦀 *braid* 🦀 *lampshade frame*
🦀 *bias cotton lampshade tape* 🦀 *spray adhesive*
🦀 *craft glue* 🦀 *clothes pins*

Make a lampshade pattern to match the lamp frame selected, following instructions above. Cut out pattern and position on frame to check accuracy. Cut pattern from thin cardboard, adding ⅜ inch to top and bottom edges and ⅜-inch overlap along one straight edge. Spray-glue cardboard to wrong side of fabric, cut around the cardboard, adding ⅜-inch allowance to top and bottom edges and along one straight side.

Fold fabric side seam allowance to wrong side and glue in place. Fold under top and bottom fabric seam allowances and glue in place, carefully clipping across seam allowances to allow them to lie flat.

Fold the bias tape in half lengthwise over top ring of lampshade. Glue tape onto ring, clipping at struts *(see diagram, page 78)*. Repeat to cover bottom ring.

Place lampshade over frame and glue side with turned fabric allowance over raw edge. Clothes pin in place until glue dries.

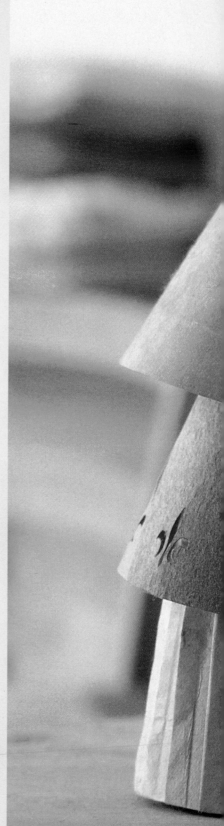

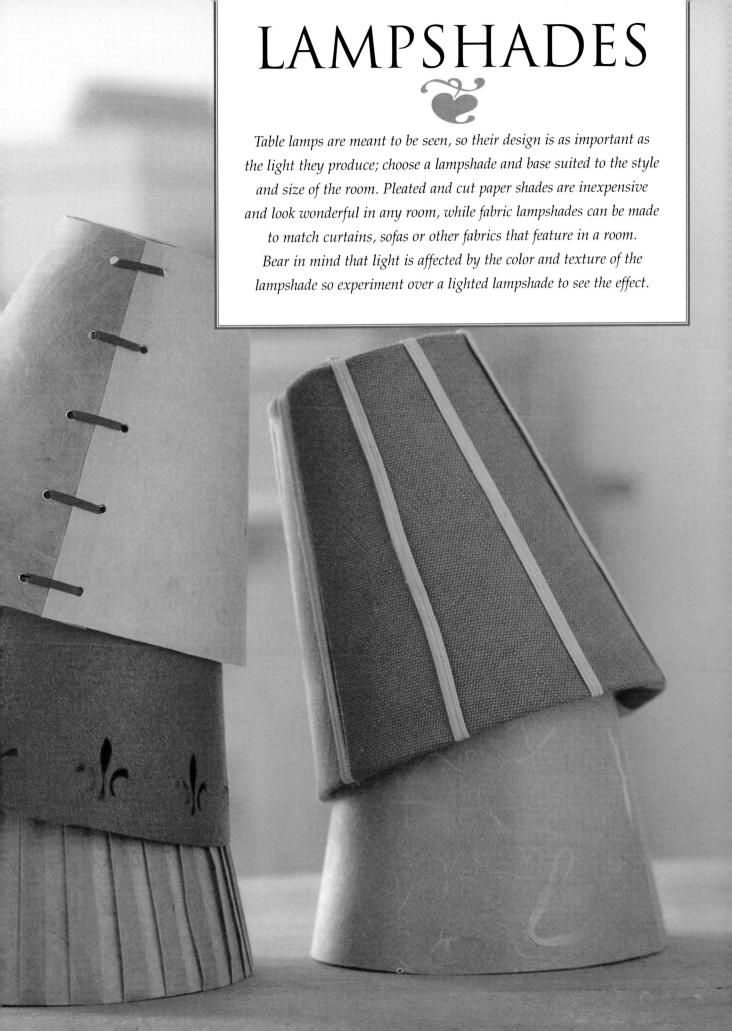

LAMPSHADES

Table lamps are meant to be seen, so their design is as important as the light they produce; choose a lampshade and base suited to the style and size of the room. Pleated and cut paper shades are inexpensive and look wonderful in any room, while fabric lampshades can be made to match curtains, sofas or other fabrics that feature in a room. Bear in mind that light is affected by the color and texture of the lampshade so experiment over a lighted lampshade to see the effect.

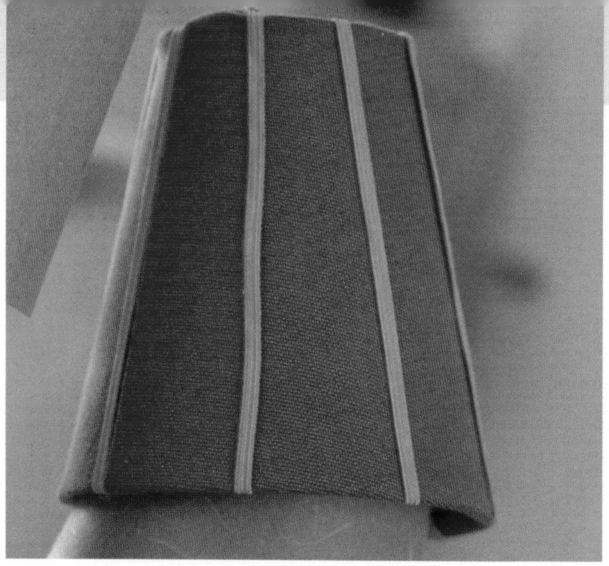

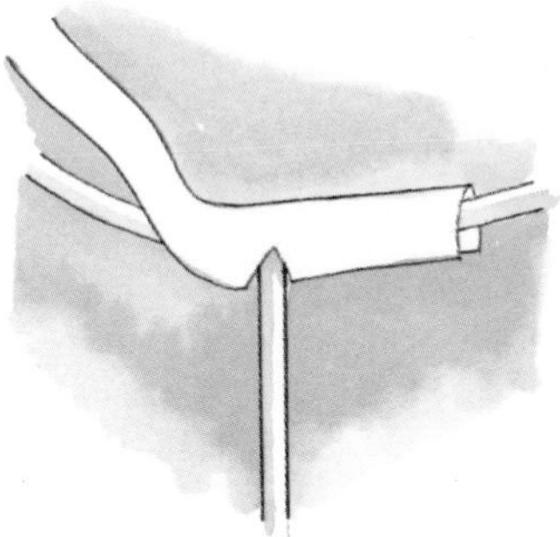

Remove lampshade from frame. To position braid, divide top and bottom circumferences of lampshade into equal sections. Cut lengths of braid 2 inches longer than height of lampshade and glue in place, as photographed, turning over 1 inch at top and bottom.

Apply glue to top and bottom rings, then place completed lampshade over frame.

Handmade Paper Lampshade

heavy paper
mulberry paper (handmade paper)
lampshade frame · *spray adhesive*
craft glue · *clothes pins*

Make a lampshade pattern to match the lamp frame selected, following instructions on page 76. Cut out pattern and position on frame to check accuracy. Cut pattern from heavy paper, adding 3/8 inch to top and bottom edges and along one straight edge. Spray-glue heavy paper to mulberry paper, then cut around heavy paper, adding 3/8-inch seam allowance to top and bottom edges and along one straight edge.

Fold mulberry paper under 3/8 inch at straight edge and 3/8 inch around top and bottom edges.

Apply glue to top and bottom rims of lampshade frame. Place lampshade around frame and glue straight edge with turned-under mulberry paper over "raw" edge, using clothes pins to keep ends in place until dry.

French Lily Lampshade

blotting paper · *heavy paper*
lampshade frame · *spray adhesive*
craft glue · *tracing paper*
blade or Xacto knife · *clothes pins*

actual size

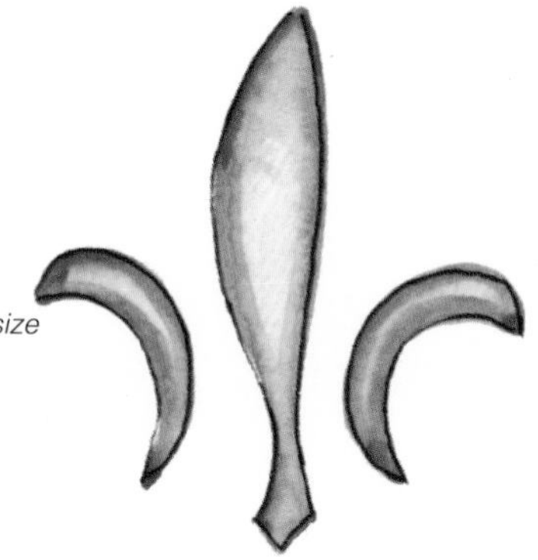

Make pattern for the lampshade to match the lamp frame selected, following instructions on page 76. Spray-glue blotting paper onto heavy paper, then cut pattern from this layered paper, adding 3/4 inch for overlap along one straight edge, 1/4 inch to top edge and 3 inches to bottom edge. Position lampshade around frame, check fit, trim if necessary.

Trace the French lily onto tracing paper and transfer to the inside of the lampshade. Space the lilies evenly around the lampshade, with each lily 1/2 inch from the bottom edge, and making sure the lilies on either side of the overlapping edge are evenly spaced. Using a craft blade or Xacto knife, carefully cut out the lilies.

Run glue along top and bottom rings of frame and along one straight edge of lampshade. Place lampshade around frame and hold in place with clothes pins until glue is dry.

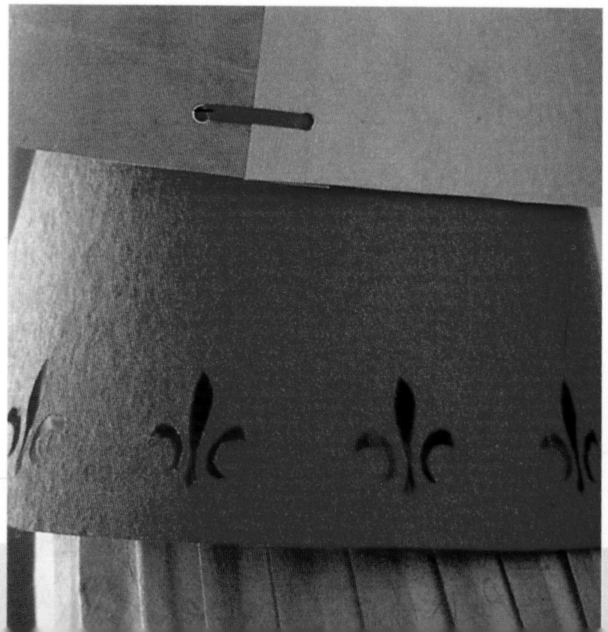

Fixed-pleat Lampshade

🐋 *heavy paper* 🐋 *thin tissue paper*
🐋 *lampshade frame* 🐋 *thin cardboard*
🐋 *spray adhesive* 🐋 *craft glue* 🐋 *clothes pins*

Make lampshade pattern to match the lamp frame selected, following instructions on page 76. Cut from heavy paper, adding ⅜ inch to top and bottom edges and ¾ inch overlap to one side edge. Make another pattern two and a half times the length of first pattern, adding 1 inch around all edges *(see diagram 1)*. Cut from thin tissue paper.

Measure finished height of lampshade and use thin cardboard to make a template of the shape of the pleat, approximately ¼ inch wide at the top and ⅜ inch wide at the bottom *(see diagram 2)*. Use the template to mark the foldlines of the pleats on the tissue paper, then fold the pleats into position. Place the heavy paper piece over the pleated section, making sure pleats at side edges are parallel to edges. Trim around piece so that there is ⅜-inch allowance along top and bottom edges and one side edge.

Spray-glue pleated tissue paper to heavy paper. Glue under ⅜ inch on side and top and bottom edges.

Apply craft glue to top and bottom rings of frame. Place pleated shade around frame, glue edge with folded paper over "raw" edge, overlapping ¾ inch. Hold lampshade in position with clothes pins until glue is dry.

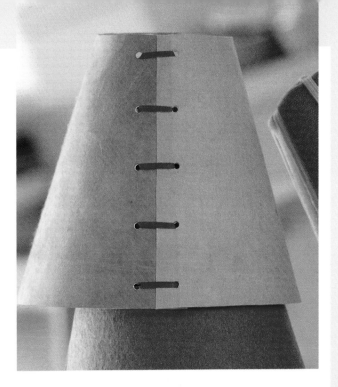

Two-colored Lampshade

🐋 *blotting paper in two different colors*
🐋 *heavy paper*
🐋 *lampshade frame* 🐋 *thin ribbon*
🐋 *spray adhesive* 🐋 *craft glue*
🐋 *hole punch* 🐋 *clothes pins*

Make a lampshade pattern to match the lamp frame selected, following instructions on page 76. Cut out pattern and position on frame to check accuracy. Divide the lampshade pattern into two equal sections, adding on ¾-inch overlap to one straight edge of each section, plus ⅜ inch to top and bottom edges. From heavy paper, cut two sections. Then cut section each from orange blotting paper and yellow blotting paper. Spray-glue one heavy paper base to the orange piece and the other to the yellow piece.

Mark position for holes along the straight edges; we positioned our holes 1½ inches from the side edge on the underlap piece and ⅜ inch from the edge on the overlap piece. (Overlap the orange on one side and the yellow on the other.) Make sure holes are evenly spaced, with top and bottom holes approximately ¾ inch from top and bottom rims.

Run a line of glue along overlapping side edge of each paper piece, then place pieces around frame, remembering to overlap orange on one side and yellow on the other. Hold in place over frame with clothes pins until glue is dry. Remove lampshade from frame, punch holes, then thread ribbon through holes, gluing ends to inside of lampshade.

Apply glue to top and bottom rings of frame and place lampshade over frame.

DIAGRAM 1

DIAGRAM 2

(not to scale)

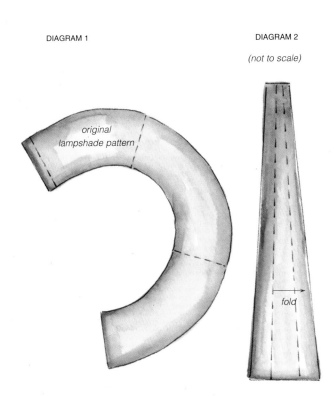

original
lampshade pattern

fold

CUT PAPER LAMPSHADE

- ❧ *heavy paper in desired color*
- ❧ *lampshade frame*
- ❧ *pencil*
- ❧ *adhesive tape*
- ❧ *craft blade or Xacto knife*
- ❧ *craft glue*
- ❧ *clothes pins*

Make a paper pattern following instructions on page 76. Add ⅜ inch for overlap along one straight edge of pattern. Add ¼ inch to top edge and 1 inch to bottom edge of pattern.

Mark a scalloped line around bottom edge of pattern, using a glass as a guide to draw the semi-circles, and beginning and ending at deepest point of scallop. Cut out pattern.

Tape pattern onto heavy paper, cut around pattern.

Lightly pencil in lily design *(see diagram)* on paper lampshade in desired positions. Using a craft blade cut along each line, being careful not to cut out any paper pieces.

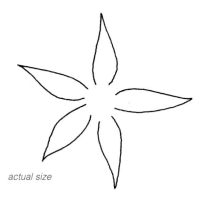

actual size

Position paper lampshade around frame, check fit and trim if necessary. Run a line of glue along top and bottom rings of frame and along one straight edge of lampshade. Place lampshade around frame, trim end scallop if necessary. Clothes pin in position until glue is dry.

BOUND FABRIC LAMPSHADE

- ❧ *thin cardboard*
- ❧ *fabric*
- ❧ *lampshade frame (we used tapered drum frame)*
- ❧ *bias cotton lampshade tape*
- ❧ *spray adhesive*
- ❧ *craft glue*
- ❧ *clothes pins*

Make pattern for lampshade to match your frame following instructions on page 76. Add ⅜-inch overlap on one straight edge of pattern, then cut pattern out. Position pattern around frame and check accuracy. Cut pattern in cardboard.

Spray-glue cardboard to wrong side of fabric, positioning cardboard to suit fabric pattern. Cut fabric around cardboard, adding ⅜-inch allowance on one straight edge.

Fold ⅜-inch allowance to wrong side, glue in place.

Fold bias tape in half lengthwise over top lampshade ring. Glue tape onto ring and clip tape at struts (**see diagram**, Lampshade with Braid Trim, page 78). Repeat to cover bottom ring.

Cut a 1½-inch-wide bias strip of fabric. Fold in half lengthwise and glue over tape-covered top ring, overlapping ends of bias.

Apply glue to top and bottom rings, and run a line of glue along lampshade edge with turned fabric allowance. Place lampshade around frame, glue edge with turned fabric allowance over raw edge. Hold in place with clothes pins until dry.

Trim any excess or uneven edges of cardboard at top and bottom of frame. To finish top and bottom edges, glue braid or a bias strip in place, turning under raw edge of overlapping end.

LINED LAMPSHADE

- 45"-wide fabric and lining coordinating fabric for bow (optional)
- ½"-wide cotton lampshade tape
- wire lampshade frame with straight sides
- thread
- long needle
- craft glue
- small paintbrush and toothpick

To make a pattern for your cover, follow instructions on page 76. Add 2 inches to top and bottom edges and 2 inches at each end for seam allowances, and cut out pattern.

Starting at a strut, wind cotton tape around upper and lower edges of frame, gluing at the start and finish to secure (see diagram 1).

DIAGRAM 1

Press fabric and lay on a smooth surface. Place pattern with its center on the diagonal and cut out fabric. Repeat for lining (see diagram 2).

DIAGRAM 2

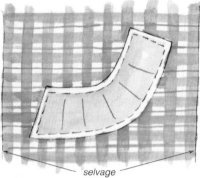

selvage

With wrong side outwards, drape the arc of main fabric around frame and pin seam edges together over a strut, making sure allowances at top and bottom edges are approximately equal and fabric overall is smooth. Slide fabric upwards and off frame.

Repeat this process for lining.

Stitch along pinned seamlines and cut away seam allowances to ¼ inch. Press to one side.

With wrong side facing outwards, slide lining up and into frame, positioning seam in line with a strut and making sure allowances at top and bottom are about equal. Pin fabric at seamline through the tape at top and bottom, stretching seam as you do so. Position fabric around inside of frame, stretching, adjusting and pinning to top and bottom rims of frame as you go.

The support struts that hold frame and lightbulb area in place will interrupt smooth pinning of these edges, so snip from the fabric edge straight in, to finish just where the strut meets the lower edge of frame. Pull fabric smoothly either side of strut and continue pinning.

Fold excess lining fabric at top and bottom down over onto outside. Once you have completed pinning, sew lining to these edges by bringing needle through from back (or inside) to outside, through all fabric thicknesses, and continue to stitch over and over around the upper and lower edges. Trim away excess lining fabric close to stitching.

Repeat this process with the main fabric, folding excess fabric after pinning over to the inside before stitching, then trimming.

Measure around upper and lower edges. Cut 5-inch-wide bias strips from main fabric to equal these measurements, plus 2 inches. Press strips in half lengthwise, wrong sides facing. Open out strips and fold in raw edges to meet center crease, press. Crease again at center line, giving double-thickness bias strips, 2½ inches wide, that are folded along their length.

Unfold bias strips, then pin strips around top and bottom edges of frame; strips should fit tautly. Remove from frame and join ends following instructions on page 125. Cut away excess fabric from seam.

Re-fold bias strips and stretch them over appropriate lampshade edge, having center crease level with edge.

Smooth and adjust binding, then lightly glue binding to shade inside and out, using a small paintbrush. Use a long needle or toothpick with small amounts of glue on its tip to reach difficult places.

Tie a tape measure into a bow to ascertain length of bow to be stitched to outside of shade or around the neck of lamp base. Cut bow (from either the main fabric or coordinating fabric) from this length of fabric by twice the desired width, plus ¾ inch for seam allowances.

Fold strip of fabric for bow in half lengthwise, right sides together, cut ends at an angle, then stitch around raw edges, allowing a ⅜-inch seam and leaving a gap at the center for turning. Turn right side out, slip-stitch opening closed. Press and tie into a bow. Stitch to lampshade, as desired.

between each line. Fold along the first line, using a ruler to give a neat crease and making sure fold is at right angles to paper edge.

Make the next crease at the dot between the lines, changing the direction of the pleat so that the lamp will be pleated "concertina fashion". Continue making ¾-inch-wide pleats along the wallpaper *(see diagram 1)*.

DIAGRAM 1

Punch a hole in the center of each pleat, 1 inch in from top edge. Repeat along bottom edge, punching holes 1½ inches in from bottom edge.

Overlap and glue the ends of pleated cover neatly together so that one end sits inside a finished pleat. Allow glue to dry before continuing. Thread the cord through the top edge holes and pull up to fit the top ring. Stitch cord ends together securely. Repeat for bottom edge.

Using double thread, attach the top edge cord to the frame by whipping over the cord between each pleat and over the ring *(see diagram 2)*. Keeping the thread taut, work all around the ring and fasten off by stitching thread to the tape. Make sure the pleats are placed evenly. Attach the lower edge to the bottom ring in the same way.

DIAGRAM 2

PLEATED PAPER LAMPSHADE

- *wallpaper (sized) or heavy paper*
- *cord*
- *lampshade frame*
- *½"-wide cotton tape*
- *strong thread*
- *leather punch*
- *craft glue*

Cut wallpaper rectangle twice the circumference of the bottom ring of the frame by the height of the shade plus 2½ inches (this allows the cover to extend 1 inch over the top edge and 1½ inches over the bottom edge).

Wrap cotton tape around the top and bottom rings of the frame (*see diagram 1*, Lined Lampshade, on page 82), hand-sew ends together.

On the wrong side of the wallpaper, lightly draw lines 1½ inches apart across the width. Mark a dot halfway

GATHERED LAMPSHADE

- ❦ *fabric*
- ❦ *lampshade frame*
- ❦ *¼"-wide elastic*

This cover is held under the bottom ring of the frame by elastic; at the top it is stitched to the ring.

Cut one piece fabric 1.5 times circumference of bottom ring, by frame height plus 4 inches, for cover. Cut one 45" x 1½" piece fabric for large tie. Cut six 4" x ⅝" pieces fabric for small ties.

Stitch short edges of cover piece together, right sides facing. Press under ¼ inch along each long edge, then press under ⅝ inch for casing on lower edge and 1½ inches for casing on top edge.

Stitch next to both folded edges of lower casing, leaving a small opening through which to insert elastic. Stitch top casing next to lower folded edge. Stitch another line ¾ inch above this row of stitching.

Clip a small hole in top edge casing at center front of cover. Hand-sew over raw edges of hole to make an eyelet.

Fold large tie piece in half lengthwise, right sides together, and stitch along 45-inch edge. Turn right side out, trim ends diagonally, fold in raw edges. Stitch across ends, press. Thread tie through eyelet in top casing. Stitch the six small ties in same way as large tie.

Place lampshade cover over frame. Pull up large tie and tie ends into a bow; tie should sit just under top ring. Hand-sew the six ties around inside top edge of cover, placing them 1 inch below the top edge and evenly spaced. Knot each tie onto top ring.

Whip-stitch top casing to top ring along upper stitching line of casing. Insert elastic through bottom casing and pull up to fit under bottom ring. Stitch ends together, slip-stitch opening closed. Distribute gathers evenly.

TIE-TOP CURTAINS

☙ *fabric* ☙ *thread*

These curtains are photographed with triple pinch pleats, but instructions are also provided for curtains that are faced and gathered through tying.

Measure finished length of curtains from bottom of curtain rod, add 8 inches for bottom hem and 1½ inches for top seam allowance if using pinch pleat header tape or ⅝ inch if making faced curtains. Calculate width as per "Measuring" on page 88. Cut fabric into required lengths. For faced curtains, cut 3-inch strips across width of fabric for top facings.

Cut strips for ties that are required length plus 1½ inches for seam allowances, and double desired width plus ⅜ inch. To determine number of ties: for pinch pleat curtains, position one pair 1 inch from each end with remaining pairs corresponding with pleats; for faced curtain, position one pair at each end of curtain with remaining pairs spaced at 6- to 8-inch intervals.

Fold each tie strip in half lengthwise, right sides together. Stitch long raw edge and diagonally across one short edge. Turn right side out, press.

For pinch pleat curtains, stitch a 1-inch double hem (see page 127) on each side. Turn under 1½ inches along top edge. Pin ties in position, with raw edges aligning with raw edge of top hem. Stitch heading tape over this hem on wrong side, following instructions for Curtain with Triple Pinch Pleats on page 93, and securing ties in stitching.

For faced curtains, press under a 1-inch double hem on each side of each curtain drop. Turn under one long edge of each facing piece, press and stitch hem. If lining curtains, leave both long edges raw (see page 88).

Open outside hem of curtain and pin a pair of ties with raw edges even against top edge, 2 inches from raw side edge *(diagram 1)*. Continue to pin pairs of ties to right side of top edge of curtain, and machine baste. Press side hem back so that all thicknesses rest on top of ties *(diagram 2)*.

DIAGRAM 1

2 inches

DIAGRAM 2

right side

fold

fold

WINDOW DRESSING

Window treatments offer privacy, insulation from noise and temperature, and protection from harsh light, as well as being decorative features. Choose a fabric and style that go with the room: a heavy tapestry drape for a lavish dining setting; a colored canvas blind for a bright, busy kitchen; a filmy white lace curtain for a romantic bedroom; or vivid chintz drawn into a balloon shade for a comfortable sitting room. Seek professional advice when selecting from the myriad header tapes, blind cords, tracks and rods, and always be prepared to experiment with non-upholstery fabrics for an individual look.

Pin facing onto curtain and ties, with raw edges even and right sides together. Trim facing so that it does not extend beyond pressed side seam. Stitch facing to curtain at top edge through all layers, understitch (see page 127).

Turn facing and side hems to wrong side so that ties are free at upper edge. Stitch side hems (see diagram 3).

For both pinch pleat and faced curtains, fold and press a 4-inch double hem at bottom edge. Insert weights and stitch.

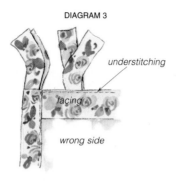

DIAGRAM 3

understitching

facing

wrong side

Adding an optional "loose lining"

Cut lining to finished length of curtain plus 3½ inches, and 4 inches narrower than width of curtain. Stitch a 1-inch double hem on side hems of lining. Once facing is attached to curtain top, stitch right side of lining to right side of bottom edge of facing, making sure side edges of lining just touch inner folds of curtain side hems (see diagram 1). Turn facing and side hems to wrong side, stitch curtain side hems, but avoid catching lining (see diagram 2). Hem lower edge of lining 1 inch shorter than curtain; top of lining hem should align with top of curtain hem.

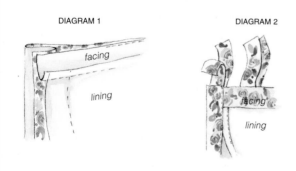

DIAGRAM 1

facing

lining

DIAGRAM 2

facing

lining

Adding an optional enclosed lining

Cut lining to finished length of curtain minus 1½ inches, and 4 inches narrower than width of curtain. Once facing is attached to curtain top and trimmed, stitch right side of lining to right side of facing at lower edge (sides of lining and facing should align.) Stitch side hems, enclosing sides of facing and lining. Turn up a 4-inch double hem at bottom of curtain, enclosing lining. Insert weights, stitch.

CURTAIN BASICS

Measuring

To estimate the finished length of a curtain, measure from the top of the rod or track to where the curtain will fall (see diagram). This length will vary depending on whether the curtain falls to the sill or floor (a), is fitted into the window recess (b) or runs from halfway down the window to the sill, as in cafe curtains.

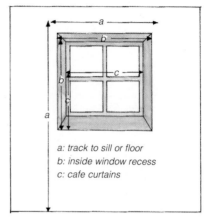

a: track to sill or floor
b: inside window recess
c: cafe curtains

Add hem and header allowances for each fabric length (these will vary according to type of header tape and whether curtain is to be hung from above or below the track). If falling to the floor, allow ⅜ inch less for stiffer fabrics so that fabric clears the floor, or a few inches more for lighter weight fabrics to achieve a "pooling" effect.

For fabric with a repeating pattern, measure the distance between one pattern and the next pattern repeat (say, 24 inches). Divide drop measurement that you have already calculated (say, 88 inches) by this number. Round resulting figure (3.6) up to the nearest number (4). Multiply this figure by the size of the pattern to obtain new drop measurement (24 x 4 = 96 inches). Now calculate how many drops you need for the fullness you require.

To estimate the finished width of curtains, measure the width of the rod or track (if it is curved and sits out from the wall, include the extra distance around the curve). For most header styles, multiply the finished width by two to allow for fullness in medium-weight or heavyweight fabrics, and triple the width for sheer or lightweight fabrics (this will vary with different headers).

It may be necessary to join fabric widths to achieve the desired fullness. Work out how many widths of fabric are required by dividing the width of the curtain by the width of the fabric. Calculate the number of panels you will need, being careful to allow extra fabric when matching patterns.

To estimate the overall fabric required for curtains, multiply the length of each fabric piece by the number of widths required.

Tracks and rods

Like header tapes, tracks and rods come in a variety of styles, ranging from flexible tracks to decorative wooden rods. Most tracks come in metal and plastic and can be bought in a range of colors.

Choose a simple track if a cornice or valance is to be fitted, as it will be concealed. For a wall-fitted track the curtains can conceal the track, if desired, or hang below the track, depending on the type of header chosen.

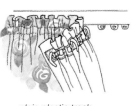

plain plastic track

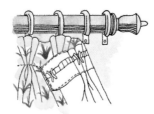

decorative rod

Weights

Weights are used in bottom hems of curtains to give shape and hold lower edges of curtains in place. The major choice of weights is between a continuous string, or weight tape, that is slipped into the bottom hem, and large circular weights that are stitched to the curtain corners. The string of weights is used for sheer or lightweight fabrics, while the individual weights are used in heavier fabrics.

Weights should be placed in each corner and on the vertical seam of every panel. When weighting unlined curtains, cover the weight before sewing it to the corner of the hem. In lined curtains the lining should hang over the weight. For curtains with a loose or detachable lining, place the weights in the curtain only, not the lining.

Header tapes

Header pleating tapes have superseded time-consuming hand-worked headers. They can form gathers, pinch pleats, pencil pleats and many other header styles. Choose the style of header tape before buying fabric, as it will influence the amount of fabric required. Tapes have cords that are pulled to form pleats or gathers, or slots through which to insert pronged hooks, which pleat the fabric.

Header tape is usually attached about ¾ inch below the top of the curtain to give the header shape and stiffness. Cut header tape 1 inch longer than fabric width. Knot cords on wrong side of one end of tape. Turn under raw

standard tape

pencil pleat tape

triple pinch pleat tape

edges of tape. Pin and stitch tape across top of curtain. Pull up cords to give desired effect and wind cords into a figure-eight, knot and leave uncut to allow for readjustment and laundering.

Hooks

Hooks are used to attach the curtain to the track; they are slotted into header pleating tape and runners. Some hooks are also used to create pleats in a curtain or add stiffness to curtain headers. Hooks are generally metal or plastic and come in a variety of sizes and styles to go with tapes.

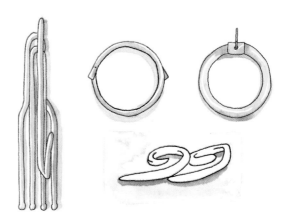

Runners

There is usually a particular type of runner than goes with each style of track. Runners range from plastic ones that slide along the track, to wooden or brass rings that are used on a decorative rod. They often have eyes through which the curtain hooks are attached. Cafe curtain rings may have clips that expand to hold the curtain, or eyes that can be stitched through.

When calculating the number of runners needed, allow one runner for each 4 inches of fabric width and an extra one for each outer end of the curtain.

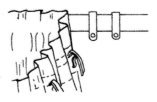

Linings

Linings protect fabric from fading in strong light, and insulate against heat, cold and noise. Cottons, calico and sateens are the most often used lining fabrics; fabrics coated with insulating materials are also available. It is best to make the lining as full as the curtain, so calculate your fabric quantities accordingly. Linings usually hang approximately 1 inch shorter than the curtain, but it is important that the top of the lining hem aligns with the top of the curtain hem.

Linings can be loose, attached or detachable. Loose lining is cut a little narrower than the curtain and made separately. It is then stitched at the top of the curtain together with the header tape.

loose lining

Attached lining is stitched together with the curtain at the side seams and top, and left free at the bottom edge. Finish the lining and curtain hems and press side hems of curtain. Place curtain and lining together, wrong sides facing, tuck sides of lining under curtain side hems, pin or baste. Stitch down curtain side hems. Finish heading as desired.

Detachable lining has header tape and hooks that attach to the main curtain tape. Convenience when laundering is the main advantage of detachable lining.

detachable lining

VOILE CURTAINS WITH RIBBON TIES

❧ *voile, or similar sheer fabric*
❧ *thread*
❧ *curtain rod with rings*

Measure the width of the window and multiply this measurement by three for the finished width of the curtain. Calculate the desired length of the curtain, remembering that with thin fabrics such as voile it is best to make the curtains over-long, to allow for a slight "pooling" of fabric. Measure length of curtain drop from the ring to the floor, adding 30 inches for the drape, 4 inches for the hems and a couple of extra inches for the pooling effect, as desired.

Cut required number of lengths for curtains, then cut a 3" x 13" tie for each ring.

With right sides together, stitch the curtain drops together along the selvages, forming one large panel of the desired width. Press under ¾ inch on each side edge and stitch close to selvage. Press under ½ inch on lower edge, then press under another 2 inches and stitch hem in place. Press under ½ inch on top edge, then press under another 1 inch and stitch in place.

With right sides together, fold tie strips in half lengthwise, and stitch long edge and one short end, allowing ⅜-inch seams. Turn ties right side out.

Position the ties in pairs, with a tie in the same position on both the front and back of the curtain, approximately 30 inches from the upper edge, and making sure the raw edge of each tie is pointing towards the top of the curtain *(see diagram 1)*. Position the outer pairs 1 inch from the outer edges of curtain, and arrange the remaining pairs of ties at even intervals of approximately 28 inches.

Stitch the ends of the ties, stitching both ends of the back and front ties to curtain at the same time. Fold the ties over so that they point towards the top of the curtain and stitch a small square to hold each pair of ties *(see diagram 2)*.

Attach the finished curtain to the curtain rings by tying or knotting each pair of ties to a ring on the rod.

DIAGRAM 1	DIAGRAM 2

CURTAIN WITH GATHERED HEADER

☙ fabric (lightweight or medium-weight)
☙ thread ☙ gathering tape

Note: Gathering tape is the standard and simplest style of header tape available. The tape produces soft gathers and is most often used on informal and unlined curtains and for small windows. Gathered headers are also used when a cornice or valance will conceal the curtain top. Gathering tape is not suitable for heavy fabrics.

Gathering tape is usually positioned ¾ inch or 1 inch from the top edge of the curtain.

For most gathering tapes the fabric should be 2.5 times the width of the track plus 2 inches for each side hem. For length, add 1½ inches allowance for header at top of curtain as well as 8 inches for bottom hem.

Turn under and stitch a 1-inch double hem (see page 127) along each side of curtain. Turn under and stitch a 1½-inch hem at top edge of curtain.

Pin tape over hem at top edge of curtain. Fold under raw ends of tape. Knot cords together at back of tape, on one end of curtain. Stitch tape in position *(see diagram 1).*

DIAGRAM 1

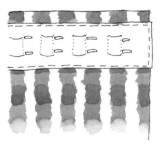

Pull up cords at unknotted end to form pleats. Wind cords into a figure-eight and knot, leaving them uncut *(see diagram 2).*

DIAGRAM 2

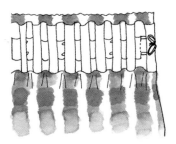

Turn under and stitch a 4-inch double hem on bottom edge of curtain.

CURTAIN WITH PENCIL PLEATS

fabric *pencil pleat tape* *thread*

Note: Pencil pleat tape forms stiff pleats, and comes with two or three alternative positions for the hooks so that they can be adjusted to suit type of track and length of curtain.

Fabric width should be 2.5 times width of track plus 2 inches for each side hem. For length, add 1½-inch allowance for header at top of curtain as well as 4 inches for bottom hem.

Turn under and stitch a 1-inch double hem (see page 127) along each side of curtain. Turn under and stitch a 1½-inch hem at top edge of curtain.

Pin tape over top hem. Fold under raw ends of tape. Knot cords together at back of tape, on one end of curtain *(see diagram 1)*.

Stitch tape in position. Pull up cords at unknotted end to form pleats *(see diagram 2)*. Wind cords into a figure-eight and knot, leaving them uncut *(see diagram 3)*.

Turn up 2 inches then 2 inches again on bottom edge of curtain, then stitch double hem in place.

DIAGRAM 1

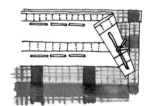

DIAGRAM 2   DIAGRAM 3

CURTAIN WITH TRIPLE PINCH PLEATS

fabric *pinch pleat tape* *thread*

Note: Pinch pleat tapes create formal, stylish curtains that are usually hung from a rod with rings or attached to a track. They have either cords that are pulled to form pleats *(see diagram 1a)*, or slots in which to insert pronged hooks that fold the fabric into triple pleats *(see diagram 1b)*.

DIAGRAM 1a   DIAGRAM 1b

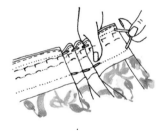   

The fabric should be 2.5 times the width of the pole or track, plus 2 inches for each side hem. For length, add 1½-inch allowance for header at top of curtain as well as 4 inches for bottom hem.

Turn under and stitch a 1-inch double hem (see page 127) along each side of curtain. Turn under and stitch a 1½-inch hem at top edge of curtain.

Fold under raw ends of tape. Pin tape over top edge hem of curtain. Leave approximately 1 inch unpleated at either side of curtain.

If using corded tape, knot cords together at back of tape on one end of curtain *(see diagram 1, Curtain with Pencil Pleats, left)*. Stitch tape in position and complete as for Curtain with Pencil Pleats. If using slotted tape, stitch tape in position and insert pronged hooks.

Turn up a 2-inch double hem on bottom edge of curtain, then stitch in place.

CURTAIN WITH CASING

❦ *fabric* ❦ *thread*

Note: If you wish to make gathered curtains but your chosen fabric is too heavy for gathering tape, a cased header is a good alternative.

Measure curtain length from above the curtain rod at desired height of header top; add 4-inch allowance for header and casing, and 4 inches for bottom hem. Fabric width should be twice the width of the rod, plus 2 inches for each side hem.

Turn under and stitch a 1-inch double hem (see page 127) along each side of curtain.

Turn under ½ inch then 3½ inches on top edge. Stitch hem in place and stitch a second row 2 inches above the first row, to form a casing *(see diagram)*.

Turn under and stitch a 2-inch double hem on bottom edge of curtain.

CURTAIN WITH SCALLOPED HEADER

❦ *fabric* ❦ *thread* ❦ *cardboard*
❦ *water-erasable marking pen or tailor's chalk*

Note: An inverted scallop header is usually used for cafe curtains but looks equally as good for long curtains with large curtain rings either sewn or clipped on.

To calculate the amount of fabric required, measure the desired length for curtain from below rod, adding 4 inches for header and 4 inches for bottom hem. Calculate desired curtain width and add 2 inches at each side for hems.

Turn under and stitch a 1-inch double hem (see page 127) along each side of curtain.

Turn under ¼ inch then ½ inch and stitch a hem on top edge of curtain. With right sides together, fold over 4¼ inches at top of curtain, press.

Make a scalloped template by drawing semi-circles along the edge of a piece of cardboard; use a teacup as a guide. Our semi-circles were 3½ inches in diameter and 1 inch apart. Use cardboard template to mark scallops along folded edge of curtain header.

Stitch along marked lines through both layers of fabric. Trim next to stitching, clip allowance *(see diagram)*. Turn right side out and press.

Clip on or stitch rings between each scallop. Turn under and stitch a 2-inch double hem on bottom edge of curtain.

CURTAIN WITH EYELET HEADER

❧ fabric ❧ fusible interfacing
❧ thread ❧ eyelets ❧ cord

To calculate curtain length, measure from approximately 4 inches below curtain rod to length desired. Add 4-inch allowance for bottom hem and ⅝-inch seam allowance at top. Fabric width should be 1.5 times the finished width of curtain plus 2-inch allowance on each side for hems. Cut a 4½-inch fabric strip the width of curtain, for header band.

Cut interfacing to same size as band and fuse to wrong side of band. Fold fabric strip in half lengthwise, right sides together, stitch across both ends. Trim seam allowance and turn strip right side out.

Stitch a 1-inch double hem (see page 127) along each side of curtain and stitch two rows of gathering along top edge. Pull up gathers to fit width of header band. With right sides together, stitch gathered edge to one long edge of header band *(see diagram)*. Trim seam allowances, turn right side out. Turn under and press allowance on remaining edge of header band. Pin and stitch band in place.

Turn under 2 inches then 2 inches again on bottom edge of curtain, then stitch double hem in position.

Attach purchased eyelets to header band, spacing them evenly, or have a bootmaker insert eyelets. Thread cord through eyelets and loop cord over rod. Knot cord behind eyelet at each end to finish.

CURTAIN WITH LOOPED HEADER

❧ fabric ❧ thread

To calculate the amount of fabric required, measure the desired width and length. Cut fabric to these measurements, adding ⅝ inch to top for seam allowance, 4 inches for bottom hem and 1½ inches to each side. Cut a 5 inch facing piece the same width as the curtain plus ⅝ inch for side seams. Cut two 6" x 3" fabric pieces for each loop.

With right sides facing, stitch two loop pieces together along 6-inch sides. Trim seam allowances, turn loop right side out, press. Make required number of loops.

Fold each loop in half across width. With raw edges of loops and top edge of curtain together, space loops evenly across curtain. Pin and stitch in place.

Turn under and stitch ½ inch then 1½ inches on each side edge of curtain and facing. Turn under and stitch a narrow hem on raw edge of facing.

Place facing and curtain right sides and raw edges together, sandwiching loops in between. Pin and stitch *(see diagram)*. Trim seam, turn right side out, press. Top-stitch across top edge of curtain, through all layers.

Slip-stitch facing to curtain at sides. Turn under raw edge of curtain then turn under a 3½-inch hem, stitch in place. Thread curtain rod through loops.

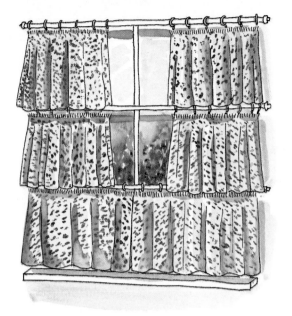

◄ When something unashamedly pretty is called for, in a child's room or bedroom, for example, "wedding cake" tiered curtains are most appropriate. Be generous with the amount of material you use; the fullness of each layer is an intrinsic part of the design's appeal. Fabric such as good-quality cotton will hang well and look fresh and crisp. These curtains have gathered headers that are attached to the rings on each of the three rods, making them easy to draw.

▼ Accentuate the shape and proportions of French doors with a pared down treatment. Diaphanous fabric is held flat against the doors by rods, top and bottom. To accentuate the simplicity of the design, each curtain is encircled by a ribbon tied in a bow at the front. A gauzy curtain fabric will allow the full circumference of the ribbon to be just visible.

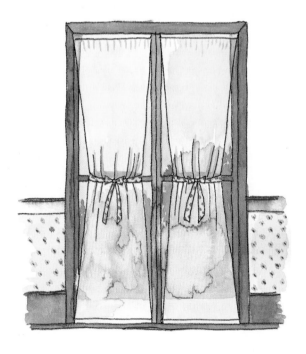

▲ The clean lines of this sublime window treatment hint at sailing away into the deep-blue yonder. The filmy, flat curtain is simply hitched up at one corner, folded back on itself and secured by a hook attached to the window frame.

CURTAINS

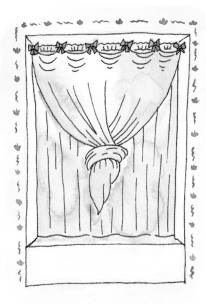

▲ Use a double layer of sheer fabric to make a theatrical statement. The bottom layer falls straight against the window while the top layer is caught into a soft knot. The header is decorated with a row of neat, contrasting bows.

▼ A plain binding in a contrasting color lends definition to a densely patterned fabric. A useful device for full-length curtains, binding adds a touch of formality. The curtain is pleated at the top and attached to rings on a rod.

▲ Exploit the film-star qualities of slinky, slippery fabric when a dramatic effect is required. These deliberately over-long drapes fall in a generous swag, are wrapped into a knot and then allowed to fall in glossy profusion to the floor. The curtains are hooked in place against the window frame, the attachment concealed by the knot.

▲ Short and sweet, this triple-pinch pleated "frieze" comprises separate short strips of curtain linked by large bows. The bows are emphasized by the use of a bold fabric design that contrasts with the curtain fabric.

Fuse interfacing to wrong side of one tie-back piece.

With right sides facing, pin then stitch tie-back pieces together, leaving a 4-inch opening on the straight edge *(see diagram 2)*. Trim seam allowances, turn tie-back right side out, press. Slip-stitch opening closed, then top-stitch ¼ inch from edge.

DIAGRAM 2

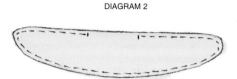

Fold each loop strip in half lengthwise, right sides together. Stitch along length, trim seam allowances and turn right side out. Turn in raw edges on ends and slip-stitch closed. Fold loops in half, stitch one on each end of tie-back.

TIE-BACKS

Make sure you adjust the length of tie-backs to fit your curtains. Heavy fabric creates extra bulk and will require longer tie-backs. Also adjust the length of the tie-back loops to fit the hooks.

Shaped Tie-Back

🐦 *½ yard x 45″-wide fabric*
🐦 *¼ yard x 36″-wide fusible interfacing*
🐦 *thread*

Finished size: 23″ x 4″.

Make pattern following *diagram 1*. Increase pattern to desired length if necessary.

Cut two tie-backs from fabric, and one from interfacing. Cut two 6½″ x 1½″ bias strips for loops. ⅜-inch seam allowance is included.

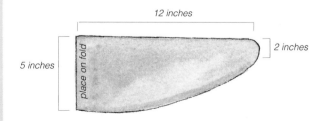

12 inches

2 inches

5 inches

place on fold

Ruffled Tie-Back

🐦 *½ yard x 45″-wide fabric*
🐦 *⅓ yard x 45″-wide contrasting fabric (for frill)*
🐦 *¼ yard x 36″-wide fusible interfacing*
🐦 *thread*

Finished size: 23″ x 6½″.

From first fabric, cut two 24″ (or desired length) x 5″ fabric pieces for tie-back. From contrasting fabric, cut one 45″ (or

twice length of tie-back; join strips to achieve this length if necessary) x 6" piece for ruffle. Cut two 8" x 1½" bias strips for loops. Cut one 24" x 5" interfacing piece (or to match tie-back). ⅜-inch seam allowance is included.

Fuse interfacing to wrong side of one tie-back piece. Trim a corner on each end into a curve *(see diagram 1)*. Trim the other tie-back piece to match.

Fold ruffle in half lengthwise, right sides together. Stitch across ends, trim seam allowances and turn right side out. Stitch two rows of gathering along raw edges of ruffle.

Pull up gathers to fit curved edge of tie-back. Evenly spacing gathers, pin and baste ruffle to interfaced tie-back piece, right sides together *(see diagram 2)*.

Pin other tie-back piece over ruffle, right sides of tie-back pieces together. Stitch all around, leaving a 4-inch opening on straight edge *(see diagram 3)*. Trim seam allowances, turn right side out, press. Slip-stitch opening closed.

Fold loop strips in half lengthwise, right sides together. Stitch along length, trim seam allowances and turn right side out. Turn under raw edges on ends and slip-stitch closed. Fold loops in half, stitch one on each end of tie-back.

DIAGRAM 1

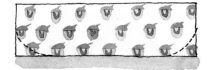

DIAGRAM 2

DIAGRAM 3

Braided Tie-Back

🌸 *⅔ yard x 45"-wide fabric*
🌸 *½ yard thick batting*
🌸 *two plastic rings*

Finished size: 29" x 3". We estimate finished length of tie-back for one drop 22–24 inches; two drops 30–32 inches; three drops 34–39 inches.

Cut three 6" x 45" (depending on width of fabric) strips of fabric. Cut three 4½" x 45" (depending on length of tie-back) strips of batting.

With right sides together, fold one fabric strip in half lengthwise and stitch long edge with a ⅝-inch seam allowance. Turn right side out. Pull a strip of batting through with a bodkin or safety pin. Repeat for other strips.

Stitch the three strips together at one end, ensuring the seams are at the back *(see diagram)*.

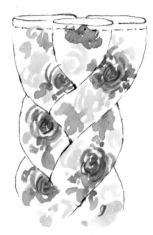

Braid finished ties until the required length is reached. Pull the braid and measure again. Cut off excess and stitch ends together.

Cut two squares of fabric to be used to bind ends. Fold each square in half, stitch folded square to end of braid, raw edges aligning. Fold in sides of square over sides of braid, then turn square to cover other side of braid end. Slip-stitch to secure. Attach a plastic ring to underside of each end (about 1 inch in from end).

edge, leaving ³⁄₈-inch seam allowance. Trim seam allowances, turn blind right side out, press. The side seams should fall on lined side of blind *(see diagram 1)*.

DIAGRAM 1

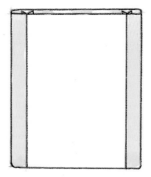

Turn up 3-inch hem at base of shade and pin along upper edge to hold in position. Cut a piece of tape same length as shade. Pin tape to lining side of shade so that it runs from ³⁄₈ inch below hem edge, along one side seamline to within ⁵⁄₈ inch of top edge of shade, positioning tape ⁵⁄₈ inch in from sides. The first ring should be about 1 inch up from hem edge. Tuck raw edge of tape under hem edge. Position other lengths of tape parallel to first tape and evenly spaced across shade (ours were 16 inches apart), tucking raw edges under hem edge. Ensure rings on tapes line up horizontally across all rows *(see diagram 2)*. Stitch tapes in position.

DIAGRAM 2

Stitch across top of hem, catching in ends of tape, to form batten casing. Insert flat batten *(see diagram 3)* and slip-stitch casing edges together.

DIAGRAM 3

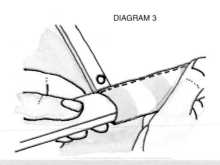

SHADES

Roman Shade

❦ fabric ❦ Roman shade tape
❦ lining fabric ❦ screw eyes ❦ fine polyester cord
❦ 2" x 1" batten, width of finished
shade, for header
❦ 1¹⁄₂"-wide flat batten, width of finished
shade, for casing
❦ staple gun or tacks ❦ cleat ❦ thread

To calculate fabric requirements, measure desired width and add 1¹⁄₂ inches at each side; measure desired length and add 2¹⁄₂ inches for top hem and 3¹⁄₂ inches for bottom hem. Cut lining piece same length as shade fabric, 2 inches narrower on each side. Mark centers at top of fabric and lining pieces.

With right sides together, match centers of shade and lining. Pin, baste and stitch along the sides and bottom

Turn under ⅜-inch allowance on blind and lining fabric along top edge, stitch. If desired, top-stitch top edge of shade 4 inches from turned-in edge.

Tack or staple fabric to top of header batten, close to the back edge *(see diagram 4)*. If necessary, adjust the position of the fabric on the header batten so that the shade fits the window exactly.

DIAGRAM 4

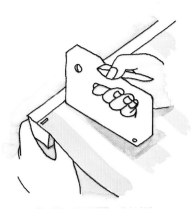

Insert screw eyes into the underside of the wooden header batten so that they line up with the rows of tape *(see diagram 5)*.

DIAGRAM 5

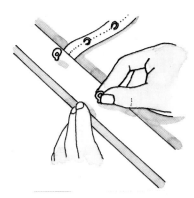

Cut lengths of cord to run the length of the shade, across the top and down one side of the shade. Knot the first length of cord to the bottom ring on one side length of tape. Thread cord through all rings on this row of tape. Repeat for other lengths of cord. Thread cords across top of shade, through screw eyes in header batten and to one side. Knot ends of cords together *(see diagram 6)*.

Mount the batten at the top of the window and attach a cleat to one side of window. Pull up shade and wind the ends of cord around the cleat.

DIAGRAM 6

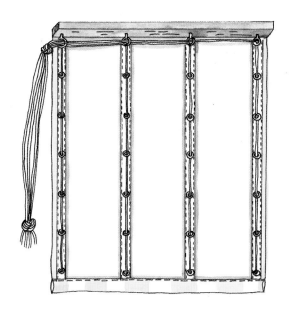

Mark the centers of fabric and backing. Place the wrong side of the fabric over the fusible side of the backing, matching centers and leaving the 1½ inches fabric allowance free on both sides.

Bond fabric to backing following manufacturer's directions. Press using a high temperature, from center of fabric to edges, and from the fabric side rather than backing side. Leave blind to cool before moving, to allow fabric and backing to bond securely.

Press 1½ inches in along both sides. Stitch 1 inch in from folded edge (we used zigzag), trim excess fabric.

If using a metal roller that has a groove to take plastic insertion, stitch top edge of shade to flat edge of plastic strip *(see diagram 1)*. If using a wooden roller, trim the top edge of shade.

DIAGRAM 1

Turn in ⅜ inch then 1½ inches on lower edge of shade for casing and stitch next to edge *(see diagram 2)*.

DIAGRAM 2

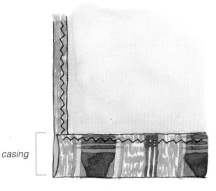

casing

Window Shade with Cut-outs

🐦 *fabric* 🐦 *fusible shade backing*
🐦 *roller and shade fittings* 🐦 *thread* 🐦 *craft blade*
🐦 *1"-wide batten, for lower edge*
🐦 *staple gun or tacks (if using wooden roller)*

To calculate fabric requirements, measure window width, subtract ⅝ inch (or less, as desired) at each side for roller fittings and add 1½ inches to each side for side hem. Measure desired length, add 2 inches for bottom casing and 12 inches for top allowance around roller.

Cut backing fabric to finished size of shade (not including side hem and casing allowances), making sure edges are straight and parallel. Use a set square to cut corner right angles accurately.

For cut-outs, mark position and shape, as desired. Zigzag around marked lines and, using a craft blade, cut out fabric inside lines.

Insert batten into lower edge of shade.

If using a metal roller, insert plastic strip into groove in roller. If using a wooden roller, tack or staple top edge of shade to roller.

Attach fittings to wall and mount shade.

Window Shade with Shaped Edge

- *fabric* - *fusible shade backing*
- *thread* - *roller and shade fittings*
- *1"-wide batten, for lower edge*
- *staple gun or tacks (if using wooden roller)*

To calculate fabric requirements, measure window width, subtract 5/8 inch (or less, as desired) at each side for roller fittings and add 1½ inches to each side for side hem. Measure desired length (to bottom of shaped edge), add 12 inches for top allowance around roller and 5/8-inch seam allowance at bottom edge. You should also allow fabric for facing and casing.

Cut backing fabric to finished size of shade (not including side hem allowances), making sure edges are straight and parallel. Use a set square to cut the corner right angles accurately.

Mark centers of fabric and backing. Place wrong side of fabric over fusible side of backing, matching centers and leaving 1½ inches fabric allowance free on both sides.

Bond fabric to backing following manufacturer's directions. Press using a high temperature, from the center of fabric to edges, and from the fabric side rather than backing side. Leave shade to cool before moving, to allow fabric and backing to bond securely.

Press 1½ inches in along both sides. Zigzag stitch 1 inch in from folded edge, trim excess fabric.

If using a metal roller that has a groove to take plastic insertion, stitch top edge of shade to flat edge of plastic strip (*see diagram 1*, Window Shade with Cut-outs, opposite). If using a wooden roller, edge-finish top edge of shade.

To make a pattern for shaped edge, take a piece of paper half the width of the finished shade and approximately 6 inches wide. Draw desired curved shape along one long edge of paper *(see diagram)*. Cut out fabric for facing piece, adding 5/8-inch seam allowance along all raw edges.

Place pattern along bottom edge of shade. Cut curved shape along shade edge.

With right sides together, pin facing over lower edge of shade. Stitch along shaped edge, trim and clip curves of seam. Turn facing to wrong side of shade.

Fold in 5/8 inch at side and top edges of facing. Stitch along long straight edge at top of facing and 1½ inches below first stitching line to form casing. Insert batten into casing. Slip-stitch edges of facing to shade.

Complete, following instructions for Window Shade with Cut-outs.

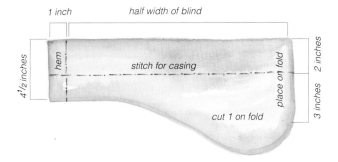

1 inch   half width of blind

4½ inches

hem

stitch for casing

place on fold

cut 1 on fold

3 inches   2 inches

Cloud Shade

- 🌿 *sheer fabric*   🌿 *fine polyester cord*
- 🌿 *⅝"-wide gathering tape*
- 🌿 *header pleating tape (we used pencil pleat tape)*
- 🌿 *⅜"-diameter plastic rings*
- 🌿 *2" x 1" batten, or balloon shade slat*
- 🌿 *curtain hooks (if using balloon shade slat)*
- 🌿 *tacks, or hook and loop tape (if using batten)*
- 🌿 *cleat*   🌿 *screw eyes*   🌿 *thread*

Note: The Cloud Shade is made from sheer fabric and has a 28-inch bottom section that remains permanently gathered. Gathering tape is stitched onto this section, cords pulled up and tied. Above the gathered section,

rings are stitched in line with the tape. These rings hold the cords that allow the shade to be pulled up and down, but remain invisible from the right side of the shade.

To calculate fabric requirements, allow 2.5 times the width of window, plus 2 inches for each side hem. Length should be 1.5 times the height of the window plus 2-inch allowance for header and 1½-inch allowance for bottom hem.

Stitch fabric lengths together using fine French seams (see page 127).

Turn under and stitch a 1-inch double hem (see page 127) along each side. Turn under 2 inches along top edge. Stitch header tape over this hem on wrong side, following instructions for Curtain with Pencil Pleats on page 93.

Turn up and press a ¾-inch double hem along bottom edge of shade, stitch.

At one side, pin a 28-inch length of gathering tape from bottom edge of blind along side hem. Position other 28-

inch lengths of tape parallel to the first tape and evenly spaced across shape (ours were about 16 inches apart). Turn under raw edges of tape and stitch in position.

Stitch rings onto shade, at 4-inch intervals, in rows from top of tape to top of shade *(see diagram 1)*. Ensure rings line up across shade.

DIAGRAM 1

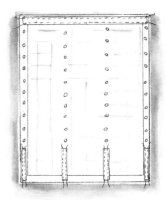

Stitch a ring into the bottom of each tape (along bottom edge of shade). Tie a length of fine cord to one ring and thread cord through rings, allowing enough length to carry it across top of shade and down one side. Repeat for each length of tape.

Pull cords in gathering tape, knot to secure. Pull cords in header tape, knot to secure.

Slip curtain hooks into header tape if using balloon shade slat.

If using a batten, fix it in position above window. Attach shade to batten with tacks, or hook and loop tape. Fix a screw eye to the batten directly above each top ring in shade. Thread cords through screw eyes and across top of shade to one side *(see diagram 2)*.

DIAGRAM 2

Attach a cleat to the side of the window where the cords are to be secured. Pull cords and secure around cleat when desired gathered look is achieved. Knot the cords together at end.

Balloon Shade

This balloon shade has a pencil-pleated header and a contrasting ruffle along the bottom edge.

- *medium-weight fabric*
- *contrasting fabric, for ruffle (optional)*
- *header pleating tape (we used pencil pleat tape)*
- *5/8"-wide gathering tape*
- *3/8"-diameter plastic rings*
- *fine polyester cord*
- *2" x 1" batten, or balloon shade slat*
- *curtain hooks (if using balloon shade slat)*
- *tacks, or hook and loop tape (if using batten)*
- *cleat*
- *screw eyes*
- *thread*

To calculate fabric requirements, allow twice the width of the window, plus 2 inches for each side hem. Length should be 2.5 times the height of the window plus 2-inch allowance for header. If not attaching a ruffle, add 1½-inch allowance for bottom hem. Ruffle strip is twice the width of shade fabric and 8 inches wide.

Stitch fabric lengths together using French seams (see page 127).

Turn in and stitch a 1-inch double hem (see page 127) along each side. Press under 2 inches along top edge.

At one side, pin a length of gathering tape from bottom edge, along side hem, to top edge of shade. Position other lengths of tape parallel to the first tape and evenly spaced across shade (ours were about 16 inches apart). Stitch tape in position.

Fold ruffle strip in half lengthwise, right sides together, and stitch along each end. Turn to right side and stitch two rows of gathering along raw edges.

Pull up gathers on ruffle to fit shade. With right sides together, pin and stitch ruffle to bottom edge of shade, leaving ¾-inch seam allowance on the shade and ⅜-inch seam allowance on the ruffle. Trim ruffle allowance, leaving shade allowance uncut.

Fold bottom edge shade allowance in half and pin flat, over ends of gathering tape and ruffle allowance. Stitch shade allowance in place.

Slip rings into tape, ensuring rings line up across shade.

Stitch header tape along top edge, over ends of gathering tape (*see diagram*), following instructions for Curtain with Pencil Pleats on page 93.

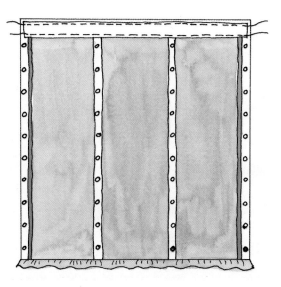

Tie a length of fine cord to each ring at bottom edge of shade and thread cords through rings. Allow enough length on each cord to carry it across top of shade and down one side.

Fix shade to batten and wall, following instructions for Cloud Shade on page 105.

CORNICES

Box Cornice

Construct a support board above window before taking cornice measurements. Cut a piece of ¾-inch-thick board so that it extends 2 inches at each side of window. Position board 2–4 inches above the window and fix with small angle brackets at each end and at regular intervals in between. Nail a square piece of board below and at right angles to each end of the long board, for end pieces.

Measure length of board including end pieces. Decide on depth of cornice, making sure it covers the support board and keeping in mind the curtain proportions. Cut fabric, lining and heavy interfacing to the required size, adding ⅜-inch seam allowance on all sides.

Trim seam allowance from interfacing, apply interfacing to wrong side of fabric, ⅜ inch in from edges.

Place lining right side together with fabric, stitch all around leaving an opening on one side. Turn right side out, press. Slip-stitch opening closed. Fold each end of fabric to fit board ends and press well to form creases.

Add trimming at this stage, if desired. Apply hook and loop tape to wrong side of cornice along top edge and along edges of support board, or tack cornice in place.

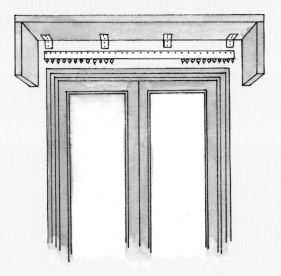

Flat Valance

A flat valance can be made easily with a straight strip of fabric, interfaced and lined as for Box Cornice. Make flat valance about 8 inches wider than window. Attach valance to the wall with hook and loop tape or tacks, allowing it to extend at each side of the window.

▼*Add a romantic touch to an otherwise plain recessed window – lace or eyelet trim is stitched to the lower edge of a flat valance. The lace extends below the valance edge to let the light filter through and further enhance the delicate framing effect of the valance.*

▲ *Scallops can softly frame a window, continue the decorative theme of a room or provide a subtle yet dramatic touch. Striped, plain or patterned, a flat valance can disguise the severe lines of a deep window recess. Variations on this theme could be zigzag edges, square cut-outs or edges cut following the pattern of the valance fabric.*

▼ *Simple elegance – a box cornice gives a decorative finish to ordinary curtains. Choose a contrasting fabric and coordinate it with tie-backs to give a more formal effect, a stylish contrast or a splash of color.*

▲ *Spirited Mexican geometrics form an innovative design for a flat valance, enlivening the outlook of a recessed window. Sunshine is drawn through the bright colours stencilled onto the fabric to create a warm and comfortable glow.*

CORNICES & VALANCES

Padded Valance

main fabric
crinoline
contrasting fabric, for backing and corded piping
piping cord
ribbon or fabric, for ties
polyester batting
wire (optional)
thread

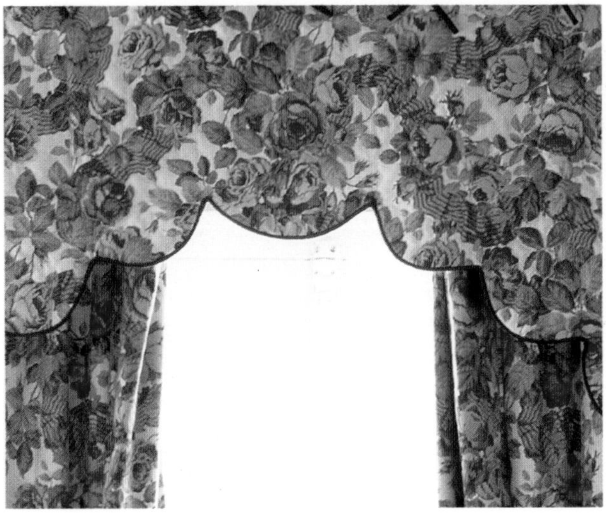

Measure the length of the curtain rod and add the distance the bracket protrudes from the wall on both sides. This is the finished width of the valance. Decide on the height and shape of the valance and make a pattern from paper. Use a dinner plate to draw the scallops.

DIAGRAM 1

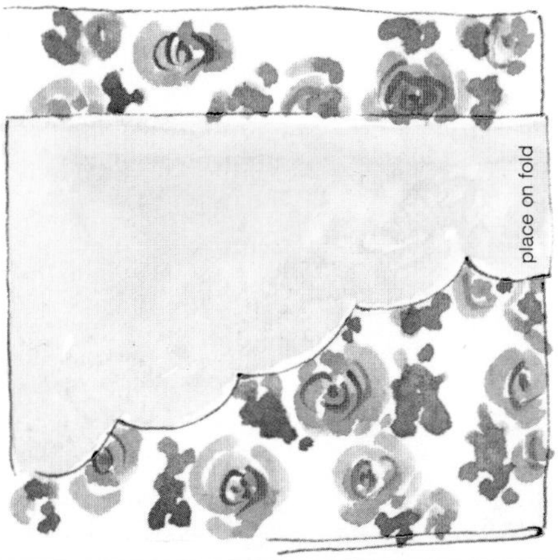

To cut fabric, fold the pattern in half and place on the fold of the fabric ***(see diagram 1)***. Add 5/8-inch seam allowance on all sides.

Cut the valance pattern from crinoline, omitting the seam allowance. Crinoline usually comes in 27-inch widths, so it might be necessary to join pieces using zigzag stitch. Cut the valance pattern from the main fabric (for front), the contrasting fabric (for backing piece) and the batting, adding seam allowances to all pieces.

Make enough corded piping from the contrasting fabric to fit around the scalloped and upper edges of the valance (see instructions on page 125). Pin the piping to the right side of the valance front, along scalloped and upper edges, with raw edges even, and place batting underneath on the wrong side of the front. Stitch in place.

With right sides together, stitch backing piece to front along the sides and just inside the piping along scalloped edge, leaving upper edge free. Understitch the side seams (see page 127) to assist the seam rolling to the back. Turn valance right side out and press.

Insert crinoline so that it sets next to the inside of the backing piece. Turn a 5/8-inch seam of the valance front to the inside, then fold 5/8 inch of the backing piece over the crinoline, trimming crinoline to fit perfectly.

Cut the required number of ties from ribbon or, if using fabric, cut required number of 12" x 1 1/4" ties. Fold fabric ties in half lengthwise, right sides together. Stitch along long raw edge and one end, allowing 1/4-inch seam. Turn ties right side out.

Tuck pairs of ties into the upper seam, between the folded edges of the front and backing piece, and pin in place. Slip-stitch backing piece to valance front along upper edge, following the piping stitching line and securing ties in stitching ***(see diagram 2)***.

DIAGRAM 2

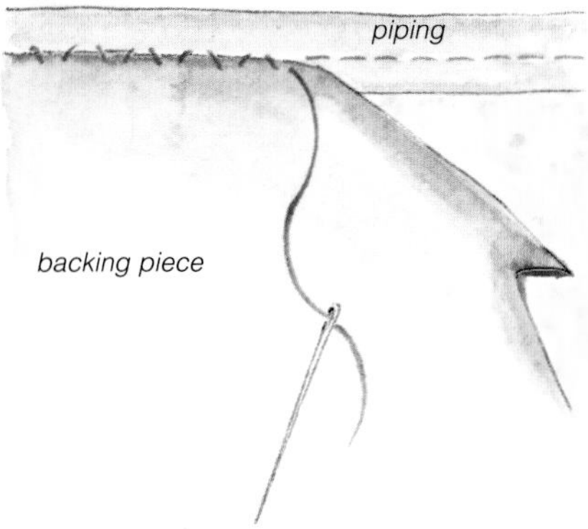

Crease the crinoline on each corner. If sharper corners are desired, insert thin wire into the back of the piping and bend into shape. Tie the ribbons or ties onto the curtain rod.

VICTORIAN THROW

🌿 *1 yard x 45"-wide patterned fabric*
(we used a tapestry-like fabric to achieve an "olde-worlde" look)
🌿 *2³/4 yards x 60"-wide solid-colored fabric, for border*
🌿 *thread*

Finished size: Approximately 50"-square; adjust the measurements to make a larger or smaller throw.

Cut the patterned fabric into a 36-inch square for the center panel. Cut the solid-colored fabric into four 8" x 60" strips for the border. ⅝-inch seam allowance is included. (To make a two-color border, sew two or three strips together to desired width, as shown in photograph).

On the center panel, mark the point at each corner where seamlines will intersect. Mark midpoint of each side and each border strip. With right sides together and matching midpoints, stitch a strip to each side of center panel, finishing stitching precisely at marked corner points. Press seam allowances towards borders. Do not trim excess fabric.

Fold the throw in half diagonally, right sides together, aligning the border seams. Mark a 45 degree angle from each marked corner point to the outside edge of the border, then stitch along marked line. Trim excess border fabric and press open seam allowances.

Cut a backing piece of solid-colored fabric the same size as the assembled front. With right sides together, pin the backing to the front, and stitch round three sides. Press seam allowances open, and turn right side out. Press in remaining raw edges and slip-stitch fourth side closed. Top-stitch all four edges, ⅝ inch in from edge.

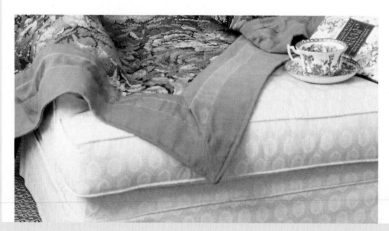

DESIGNER TRIMS

A few simple accessories complete a decorating scheme, adding a final touch of individuality or comfort. Ordinary drapes become classically elegant when tied back with tassels, and an easy-to-make throw makes a favorite sofa even more inviting. Designer accents can also be used to dress up functional objects or brighten dull areas – we show you how to turn storage boxes into decorator items with fabric and appliqué, and add a historical accent to a kitchen or hallway with a stenciled Victorian floor cloth.

COVERED STORAGE BOXES

- ❧ cardboard boxes (see **Note**, below)
- ❧ upholstery or heavyweight cotton fabric
- ❧ calico or lightweight cotton
- ❧ lightweight cardboard
- ❧ craft glue
- ❧ contrast piping, purchased, or make your own
- ❧ following instructions on page 125 (optional)
- ❧ iron-on interfacing, for appliqué
- ❧ 1½"-wide grosgrain ribbon, for decoration (optional)
- ❧ polyester fiber fill for padded appliqué
- ❧ brass card-holder (optional; see **Note**, below)

Note: Large stationery shops or specialty storage shops often have cardboard box kits in a variety of sizes. You can also use boxes scrounged from supermarkets, of course. Brass card-holders are a lovely finishing touch, and are handy for listing the contents of your boxes.

Covering box

Carefully measure sides and base of box and cut fabric pieces to match, allowing ¼-inch seam allowance and 1-inch fold-over allowance around top edge. This method allows you to match large patterns or stripes at the sides.

With right sides facing, stitch side pieces together to form a circle. With right sides together, stitch base piece to sides to form a cloth "box".

If you are using a solid-colored fabric or small print that does not need matching, place the box on the wrong side of the fabric, trace around its base and cut the base and sides from a single cross-shaped piece of fabric, remembering to add seam and fold-over allowances. Stitch the side seams, right sides together. Turn right side out.

Check that fabric fits snugly on the box, adjust if necessary. If you wish to add padded appliqué shapes, stitch them to box cover before completing the next step.

Slip box into fabric covering, stretch fabric firmly, fold allowance to inside of box edge and glue in place.

From lightweight cardboard, cut side and base panels in the same measurements as box, minus ½ inch in height.

Cut corresponding pieces of calico or lining material, allowing an extra 1 inch on all sides. Place cardboard rectangles squarely in the center of calico rectangles (on the wrong side), fold in edges and glue in place.

Glue lining panels to the inside of the box, wrong sides together, noting that panels are about ½ inch shorter than the top edge of the box.

Cover the lid in the same way as the box, but cut the lining panel cardboard to the same size as the side of the lid, not ½ inch shorter. Add piping, if desired, to the top edge of the lid, securing it in the seam. If adding piping to the lower edge of the lid, glue it in place along the edge after the outer cover has been secured; the raw edge will be concealed by the fabric-covered lining panel.

Applying appliqué

If you wish to decorate the box or lid with appliqué, choose simple shapes, such as diamonds, triangles, circles or half circles, and arrange according to taste, or follow the photograph.

Remember that flat shapes can be glued in place after the box is finished, but the padded appliqué should be stitched to the cover *before* gluing.

If using flat shapes, to prevent fraying, iron interfacing onto the wrong side of the fabric before cutting out, then glue shapes in place.

For padded appliqué, cut two pieces for each shape, allowing ¼-inch seam allowance. With right sides together, stitch around the outer edge of each shape, then carefully make a small slit in the center of one side only, and turn right side out through the slit. Stuff shape with polyester fiber fill and baste opening closed. Stitch or glue each appliqué shape in place on the box cover, with the slit to the inside. If desired, grosgrain ribbon can be added to the edge of the box or lid first, then appliqué added to the ribbon (*see photograph*).

As a final touch, add a brass card-holder to the side or end of your box.

FOOTSTOOL COVERS

Braided Footstool Cover

- *upholstered footstool*
- *fabric*
- *braid in three colors*
- *craft glue*
- *small tacks*
- *tack hammer*
- *tailor's chalk*

Measure from the lower edge of the upholstered part of the stool on one side, up and across the top and down to the lower edge on the other side. Measure the width across the top of the stool between the points where the top begins to curve downwards at the sides. Use these measurements to make a paper pattern for top cover piece.

Pin the top pattern to the stool before measuring for the side pieces. Make a paper pattern for these, leaving all the corners square.

Cut the top and side pieces from fabric, adding ⅝-inch seam allowance at the ends and upper edges of the side pieces, and to the sides of the top piece. Mark the seamlines on the wrong side of the top piece and on the right side of the side pieces.

Pin the side pieces to the stool, aligning their lower edges with the lower edge of the stool, then pin the top piece to the stool. Make adjustments if the seamlines are not matching exactly. Draw around the corner seamlines of the side pieces using the top piece seamline as a guide, take

the pieces off the stool and use a glass or plate to trim the rounded corners neatly. Trim seam allowance around corners to ⅝ inch.

With right sides together, pin top piece to sides, stitch; press seam allowances away from sides.

Cut two strips of braid (in the same color) the length of the top cover section to decorate the top of the footstool. Cut another two lengths of (different-colored) braid, each measuring the perimeter of the stool at the lower edge plus 1½ inches for overlap.

Place the cover back on the stool and pin a braid strip to the top section approximately ⅝ inch inside each seamline. Remove the cover and stitch braid in place using a zigzag setting, or, if applying a heavy braid, the embroidery or appliqué foot.

Replace the cover on the stool and begin gluing the other two braid strips to the lower edge. Starting in a corner of the stool, apply glue to small section of cover. Wait until glue is tacky, then firmly press a section of braid in place, stretching it slightly. Insert tacks invisibly at intervals. Turn under the end of the braid and glue to the cover.

Tasseled Footstool Cover

- *fabric*
- *corded, tasseled curtain tie-backs, or thick cording with tasseled end*
- *large decorative or fabric-covered button (optional)*

Measure the length and width of the stool top. Cut a paper pattern to these measurements, rounding corners slightly and marking the corner point on each seamline. Cut from fabric, adding ⅝-inch seam allowance on all sides.

Take the side length measurement from the top to 1½ inches below the lower edge of the upholstered section, or to length desired. Calculate the width of side piece by measuring around all sides of the top piece. Use this measurement plus ⅝-inch seam allowance at each end if fabric is wide enough for you to cut the sides as one continuous piece. Otherwise, measure width of each side and cut a pattern for one side if stool is square, or for two sides if stool is rectangular. Cut side piece(s) from fabric, adding ⅝ inch at upper edges and sides, and 1½ inches at lower edges. Mark the corner points on the upper edge seamline.

Stitch the ends of the side pieces together, right sides facing, to form a ring. Stitch the side piece to the top piece, matching the marked corners.

Place the cover over the stool, check the hemline. Turn under and stitch a ¾-inch double hem (see page 127).

Place the cover on the stool and arrange the cords and tassels. If using curtain tie-backs, knot them together at the center of the stool (*see diagram*) and stitch in place by hand. If using tasseled cording, cut to the desired length and drape across stool so that cut ends meet at the center of the cover top. Baste cords in place and hide the ends with a large decorative button.

Piped Footstool Cover

❧ *upholstered footstool*
❧ *main fabric, for main part of stool*
❧ *first contrast fabric, for accent stripe*
❧ *second contrast fabric, for piping*
❧ *piping cord*

Measure the top and sides of the stool, following the instructions for the Tasseled Footstool Cover, and cut patterns to finished measurements. If stool is rectangular, you will need to cut two side patterns.

Fold the top pattern in half and mark a cutting line for the center stripe. Fold one side pattern and mark in the same way, making sure the inset stripe meets with that of the top (*see diagram 1*).

DIAGRAM 1

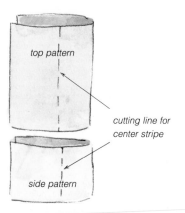

top pattern

cutting line for center stripe

side pattern

Cut along the top piece cutting line, giving patterns for center stripe and main outer section. Cut two outer sections from main fabric, and one center stripe from first contrast fabric, adding ⅝-inch seam allowance on all sides of pieces.

Cut along cutting line marked on side piece, giving patterns for inset stripe and end section. Cut four end sections from the main fabric, adding 2 inches to one side for the corner pleat, ⅝-inch seam allowance to the other side and along the upper edge, and 2-inch hem allowance. Cut two inset stripe sections from the first contrast fabric, adding ⅝-inch seam allowance to sides and upper edges, and 2-inch hem allowance.

Also cut two plain side pieces from the main fabric, adding seam, hem and pleat allowances as above.

From main fabric, cut four pleat inserts, each 5 inches wide by length of side pieces plus ⅝-inch seam allowance at the upper edge and 2-inch hem allowance at lower edge.

From second contrast fabric, cut enough bias strips to equal outer edge measurement of top cover, when joined. Make corded piping following instructions on page 125.

Stitch the top center stripe to the main outer sections, right sides together. Mark corner points on the seamline. Apply piping to the right side of the top piece following the instructions on page 125.

Make up the striped side pieces. With right sides facing, stitch the ends of the pleat inserts to the ends of the side pieces, to create a ring. Press seam allowances together.

Mark a point 2 inches from pleat insert seamline on upper seamline of each side piece. Bring points together to create corner box pleats (*see diagram 2*). Stitch pleats down about 2 inches from upper edge on wrong side (*see diagram 3*).

DIAGRAM 2

2 inches   2 inches

DIAGRAM 3

stitch down 2 inches

With right sides together, stitch top to sides, matching corners and aligning inset stripes. Place cover on footstool and check hemline. Turn under and stitch a ¾-inch double hem (see page 127).

CANVAS FLOOR CLOTH

- 45" x 60" pre-sealed artist's canvas, or ordinary canvas painted on one side with white acrylic paint
- rolls of 1-inch, 1¹/₂-inch and 2-inch masking tape
- natural sponges, for applying paint
- artist's acrylic paints in creamy yellow, deeper yellow, brick red, clear red, medium green, blue-green and yellow-green
- acetate or cardboard (see **Note**)
- linseed oil and turpentine, if using cardboard stencils
- craft blade or Xacto blade
- white PVA glue
- clear acrylic varnish, or non-yellowing oil-based varnish
- paintbrush, for applying varnish

Finished size: 41 inches x 56 inches.

Note: You can cut your stencil from clear acetate or calligraphy parchment; both materials are available from art supply shops. Or you can use two sheets of manila cardboard, abutted and then held with masking tape top and bottom.

Oil the cardboard with a 50/50 mixture of linseed oil and turpentine to make it waterproof. Mix the oil and turpentine together in a jar, shake and rub the mixture into both sides of cardboard with a soft cloth. Allow ten minutes drying time before rubbing away excess oiliness with another soft, clean cloth.

If you plan to make a larger or smaller cloth while still using the apple stencil, plot on paper first how many multiples of the stencil and widths of the masking tape you can fit, and purchase your canvas accordingly.

*Broken lines indicate
pattern repeats*

Borders

Place creamy-yellow paint into a shallow container and dilute it with a little water. Moisten a large sponge and squeeze all moisture from it. Dab sponge into paint mixture and squeeze away excess. Dab sponge lightly onto kitchen paper to avoid creating large "blobs". With canvas spread flat, gently dab sponge all over surface of canvas, creating a light stippled effect. Repeat process with deeper yellow paint. Allow to dry thoroughly before applying borders.

Study *diagram 1*, which shows positions of borders. Borders are created by laying down three strips of masking tape (from widest to narrowest) with edges abutted, then removing center strip, leaving area to be painted (*see diagram 2*). The 2-inch area between the outer border and the edge becomes the mat's hem.

Sponge shades of brick red and then clear red over the already yellow base for the borders. Remove tape strips at the side when border paint is dry. Make the outer and inner straight borders first, then the diamond-shaped section in the center panel.

When all borders are painted and dry, place tape over the painted inner straight border and the diagonal border. Sponge the four inner corner sections with a medium green first, then a blue-green, then lightly with a yellow-green. Carefully remove tape strips when dry.

Stenciling

Trace the stencil design (opposite) onto acetate sheet or cardboard and, as a guide, cross-hatch areas to be cut out. Cut out stencil using a craft blade or Xacto blade. If you taped cardboard together, cut through the masking tape as if it were not there.

Position stencil so that end of apple stem sits ¾ inch from border, and design itself appears centered between two borders. Pour a small amount of paint into a shallow container, spreading it slightly. Wet, then "dry" sponges – you need only to soften them – keeping one for reds and the other for greens. Dab the sponge into the paint and dab off any excess onto a kitchen towel.

Gently start to fill in the motifs, applying a variety of greens for the leaves, and a variety of reds for the apples. Mix red and green to make brown for the stems.

The outcome should not be uniform coverage but instead a soft speckled effect. Lightly sponge deeper or lighter shades over leaves and apples, giving a dimensional effect, remembering that the yellow background will soften the whole effect and should be allowed to show through.

Flipping stencil for each alternate motif, repeat motif three times down long sides of mat (six bunches of apples) and twice across each short end (four bunches of apples). Continue to stencil clockwise around mat, again placing stem ¾ inch from edge at short ends. At each corner, add another leaf to fill in an otherwise too-blank area.

Stencil four additional motifs in the center diamond – study the photograph for guidance – and add extra leaves to the motifs in this area.

Finishing

Turn mat over and crease edge over 2 inch, along outer border. Score along the creaseline to make sure it will set folded. Paint hem area with glue, allow to dry slightly and re-press hems into place, cutting away excess fabric at corners to reduce bulk. Some form of weight may be necessary to keep hems and corners in place while drying.

Note: The paint drying on the canvas surface can create undulations in the mat. Should this happen, spray the underside lightly with water, then paint with a 50/50 mixture of water-based glue and water. As dampness softens the canvas, smooth out the bumps and, if necessary, use masking tape down the sides to hold the mat in a smooth position until it is dry.

DIAGRAM 1

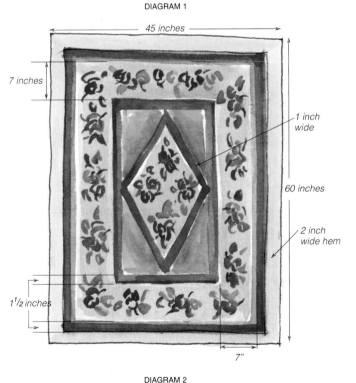

45 inches

7 inches

1 inch wide

60 inches

2 inch wide hem

1½ inches

7"

DIAGRAM 2

peel away abutted masking tape to reveal area for sponged border

TASSELS

Basic Tassels

- *small amount heavy cardboard*
- *yarn of desired thickness (see Note, below)*
- *large-eyed needle*

Note: Almost any yarn can be used to make a tassel. We used DMC Pearl Cotton No. 5. As a guide to quantities, a 1½-inch-long tassel, wound 50 times around with No. 5 Pearl Cotton, requires approximately 6 yards.

Cut a piece of cardboard, approximately 12 inches long by desired length of the finished tassel, to make a template. Wind the yarn around one end of the template until the desired thickness is achieved (about 50 times, if using Pearl Cotton), starting and finishing the yarn at the bottom of the card. This forms the body of the tassel.

Take the yarn, without cutting it, about 1 inch further along the card and start winding another tassel. Continue in this manner until the card is full ***(see photo 1).***

While the yarn is still on the card, cut a separate length of yarn about 18 inches long (one length for each tassel, if mass producing), thread it through a needle so that it becomes double, and thread it under the wound yarn at the top of the tassel, tying the ends in a firm square knot ***(see photo 2)***. This is called the holding cord.

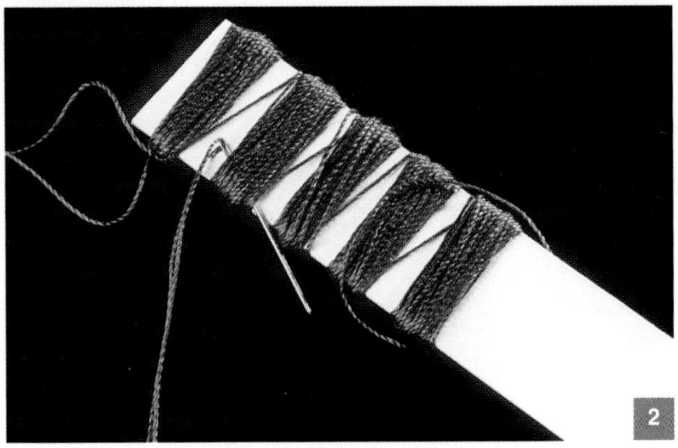

Remove each tied tassel from the card (snipping the connecting threads between). Cut another length of yarn about 12 inches long (one for each tassel) and wrap the tassel a short distance below the holding cord to form the neck ***(see photo 3)***. To keep tassels secure, tie off the loose ends, then thread with a needle behind the neck and leave them to blend with the bottom of the tassel.

Cut the loops at the bottom to form the tassel fringe.

Multiple or Family Tassel

This tassel is made with a total of 32 basic tassels – 16 x 1¼-inch tassels and 16 x 1¾-inch tassels – attached to a plastic ring that is suspended between two wrapped balls and held by a twisted cord.

✓ *heavy cardboard for templates*
✓ *DMC Pearl Cotton No. 5 (Art 116) in the following colors and amounts: 2 balls each of blue (930), red (816), gold (977) and green (991), and one ball of écru*
✓ *1 skein or spool DMC Metallic Embroidery Floss*
✓ *large-eyed needle*
✓ *1½"-diameter Styrofoam ball*
✓ *metal skewer, or other sharp tool*
✓ *large wooden macramé bead, slightly smaller than Styrofoam ball*
✓ *1½"-diameter plastic curtain ring*

Winding yarn 50 times around the template, make 16 basic tassels, each 1¾ inches long: four each of blue, gold, red and green. Make another 16 basic tassels, each 1¼ inches long: four each of red, gold, green and écru.

With metal skewer, make a hole through middle of Styrofoam ball and wrap or satin stitch it with double thread of blue No. 5 Pearl Cotton. Knot ends when finished and work them round into center hole so they cannot be seen.

Using double threads of metallic gold yarn in the needle, wrap or satin stitch decorative lines on top of the blue yarn.

Wrap wooden bead with blue yarn, as for Styrofoam ball, omitting metallic gold.

Attach the 1¼-inch tassels to the curtain ring, alternating colors, one after the other, until all are attached. Attach each tassel with a chain stitch *(see photo 1)*, then anchor thread in bar of holding cord with two buttonhole stitches (see page 126). Bury ends of holding cord by threading them through into tassel fringes and trimming off ends to match.

Lift the smaller tassels out of the way into center of the ring and attach the 1¾-inch tassels, alternating between each of the shorter tassels, forming a top row of 1¼-inch tassels and a bottom row of 1¾-inch tassels (*see photo 2*).

Make a twisted cord, approximately 20 inches long, using 4–6 lengths of blue yarn. Double the yarn by hooking it over a door knob or door handle. Twist the doubled cord between thumb and index finger until it is tightly coiled. Find the halfway point, carefully double the cord, then let it twist together in small sections, to prevent knotting.

Thread ends into a large-eyed needle and knot other end. If needle eye is too narrow to thread, simply stitch cord to eye of needle, using an ordinary needle and thread. Take needle first through Styrofoam ball, then through ring of tassels, and lastly through wooden bead.

Unthread cord and tie a large knot in bottom of cord, below wooden bead, to hold it in place.

Stitch other end back into cord to form a loop above Styrofoam ball. Snip off original knot, then knot the now-double cord and use a needle to move the knot into the hole of ball in order to conceal the stitching (*see photo 3*).

Hang completed tassel from the loop formed by the cord.

Tasseled Tie-Back

❧ *two lamp holders*
❧ *2¼ yards x ½"-diameter twisted cord*
❧ *½ yard x 6"-wide twisted fringe trim*
❧ *white kitchen string*
❧ *four metal rings to fit widest end of lamp holders*
❧ *⅓ yard x ½"-diameter braid*
❧ *solvent-based adhesive*
❧ *needle and matching thread*
❧ *tacky craft glue (water-based)*
❧ *Artist's Quality Gouache (such as Jo Sonja's):*
Rich Gold, (or color to match fringe trim)
❧ *water-based satin varnish*
❧ *paintbrush*

Unscrew lamp holder and remove black electrical piece. If hanging cord is thick, you might need to drill out the hole a little. Glue the two pieces of white casing together with solvent-based adhesive. A little sticky tape around the "seam" may help to keep the pieces in position.

Cut a 20-inch length off the twisted cord and rebind all four raw edges with sticky tape to prevent unravelling. Set shorter piece of cord aside. Using a needle and thread, bind the edges of the remaining 60-inch piece just inside the tape, stitch to secure, then cut off taped piece, leaving a neatly bound edge.

Cut twisted fringing into two 9-inch lengths. Thread one bound end of the twisted cord through the top of the lamp holder and out the bottom. (Do not thread cord through second lamp holder until first tassel is complete, as you may not be able to slide brass rings over string-covered lamp holder.) Apply solvent-based adhesive along the top of one piece of fringe trim, and roll tightly around cord (*see diagram 1*). Pin or tie to secure while drying.

DIAGRAM 1

When dry, spread a little glue around the inside lower edge of the lamp holder and pull the top of the fringe trim back inside it, until the flange on the top of the fringe trim is concealed. Allow to dry.

Spread tacky craft glue over outside of lamp holder in a thin film. Starting at the lower edge, wrap kitchen string tightly around the holder to cover it completely, keeping rows neatly and tightly together. Cut at top. When dry,

paint the string with gold acrylic paint, making sure that no white is visible. If desired, paint brass rings to match (or leave plain if you prefer the brass look). If painting rings, coat them with varnish as well.

When dry, slide two painted rings along cord and over the lamp holder from the top. Spread a little solvent-based adhesive around lower rim of holder and ease one ring down to the bottom of the holder over glue. Leave second ring free for the moment. Allow glue to dry.

Apply a thin line of adhesive just above lower ring. Take the 20-inch cord (cut off earlier) and remove the tape from one end, not allowing cord to unravel. Run cord around lamp holder next to ring, then cut cord sharply where the two ends meet. Spread both ends with more adhesive and press ends together neatly. If necessary, use a pair of tweezers to help tuck the edges together.

Spread a fine line of adhesive along the top edge of the cord and press the second ring down over holder, wedging cord firmly between rings.

Spread another line of adhesive around holder along top edge of second ring, and run a line of braid around, cutting ends to meet neatly. Run a little more braid around where the lamp holder and the cord meet (line up all cord connecting points on one side, wherever possible).

Make a second tassel on other end of cord in the same manner, but remember to slip remaining two painted brass rings onto cord before attaching lamp holder.

The cord for the tie-back can be knotted as follows: Make two loops in the cord, leaving one tassel longer than the other (*see diagram 2*). Wrap the right cord over the left (*see diagram 3*) and behind, bringing it through the center of the loops (*see diagram 4*), making sure loops are even. Wrap twice more (*see diagram 5*). Holding firmly, stitch cord together using invisible stitching to keep in place. One tassel should hang slightly below the other.

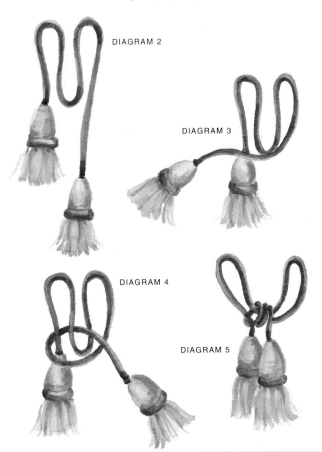

DIAGRAM 2

DIAGRAM 3

DIAGRAM 4

DIAGRAM 5

GENERAL INSTRUCTIONS

Gathering

1. Set the machine on the longest stitch length. Stitch two lines of gathering either side of the seamline.

2. Pull up gathering threads until fabric is the desired width. Distribute gathers evenly or as required.

Stitching a casing

Fold under raw edge then fold again for casing. Stitch two lines to make the casing. Casing should be at least ¼ inch wider than the cord or elastic to be threaded.

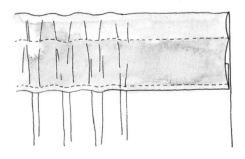

Open seam

1. Place fabric pieces right sides together. Pin and stitch at desired distance from raw edge. Knot threads at each end or backstitch to secure.

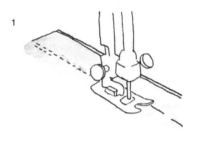

2. Neaten raw edges by zigzagging or overedging, and press open.

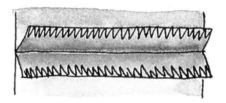

Clipping and notching a curved seam

A curved seam should be clipped or notched along the seam allowance to ensure it lies flat. Clip an outward-curving seam by making small snips in the seam allowance (a), or notch an inward-curving seam by cutting small V-shapes out of the seam allowance (b).

Making and applying bias binding

1. Fold fabric so that lengthwise and crosswise grains align (the bias is at 45 degree angle to the selvage). Cut bias fabric strips desired width.
2. Join strips to give desired bias length by stitching across straight grain. Trim next to stitching. If bias is to be used for binding, press a hem on each side of bias strip and press strip in half lengthwise.

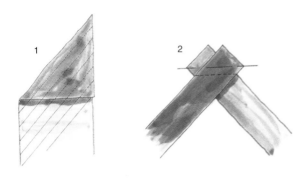

3. To bind fabric edge, align raw edges of bias strip and fabric. Stitch, and turn binding over fabric edge. Turn under raw edge of binding and slip-stitch into stitching line, or (4) machine stitch next to binding edge.

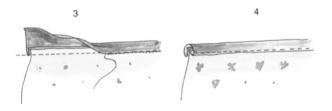

Making and applying corded piping

1. Fold bias over piping cord. Using a zipper foot, stitch next to cord.
2. Pin piping on fabric, aligning raw edges. Using a zipper foot, stitch in place.

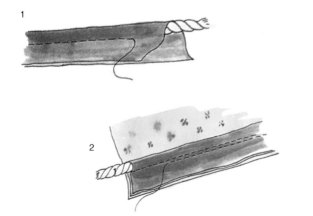

3. Pin remaining fabric piece in position. Stitch seam.
4. To apply piping around corners, clip from raw edge towards stitching. Pin piping around corner, easing to fit.

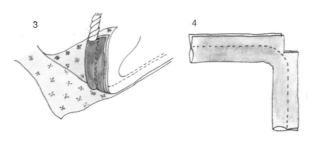

Joining piping

1. To join lengths or ends of piping, fold under the end of the fabric that covers piping. Trim and abut ends of cord. Overlap the folded fabric end over the other end.
2. Hand-stitch the fabric ends together.

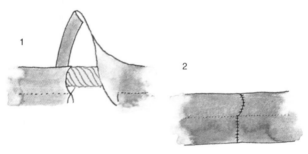

Mitering or dovetailing square corners

1. Turn seam allowances right side out and press.

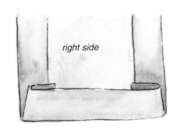

right side

2. Make a diagonal fold in the corners of the seam allowances and press, stitch along foldline. Trim seam allowances, press open, turn hem to wrong side. Press.

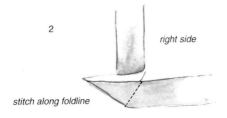

right side

stitch along foldline

Inserting a zipper

1. Measure and mark zipper position on the seamline. Baste the seam closed and press seam allowance open.
2. Place zipper face down over seam allowance, aligning zipper with seamline. Baste, then stitch around the zipper. Remove all basting stitches.

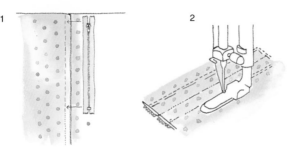

Buttonhole stitch

Backstitch

Hem stitch

Work hem stitch on wrong side from left to right. Secure thread in hem fold with a knot, bring needle through hem. Pass needle under a fixed number of fabric threads (3-4), taking needle from right to left. Pull needle through and take up two threads of hem fold to right of thread bundle.

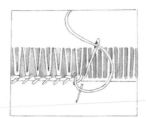

Star stitch

Work straight stitches into a central point. Stitches can be the same or varied lengths.

Stem stitch

Eyelet stitch

Pierce a small hole with large darning needle. Work close overcast stitches around the raw edge.

Satin stitch

Matching patterns

When joining fabric pieces, a more professional finish is achieved by matching the fabric pattern across the seam. To do this, move the pattern pieces up and down, next to each other, until the pattern aligns. The pattern should be matched at the level of the stitching line, rather than the cutting line.

French seam

1. Use a French seam on sheer fabrics or where the wrong side of seam will be visible. Place fabric pieces wrong sides together. Pin and stitch at a distance equal to half the seam allowance. Trim next to stitching.

1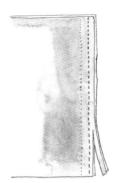

2. Fold fabrics right sides together. Pin and stitch along seamline. Press seam allowance to one side.

2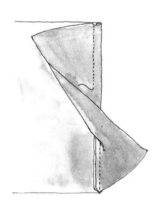

Double hem

Turn under fabric edge twice, the same amount each time. Stitch hem. This gives a stable, opaque hem, useful for curtains.

Top-stitching

Using a slightly longer stitch than usual and working from the right side of fabric, stitch parallel to the fabric edge. Heavy or contrasting colored thread can be used for a more decorative effect.

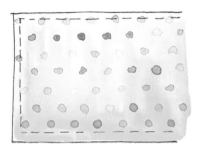

Understitching

Use understitching to prevent facings from rolling to outside, or whenever a seamline forms an edge enclosing seam allowance. Press seam allowance towards facing. From right side of facing, stitch close to seamline and through all seam allowances.

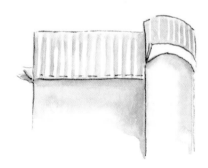

Marking a large circle

Fold fabric in half lengthwise and then in half crosswise. Tie one end of a string around a pencil and pin the other end to the fabric center. Length of string should be half the desired diameter of the circle.

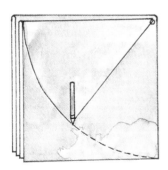

INDEX